W9-CLD-606

ENDORSEMENTS

Of the many fine monographs Ken Hemphill has written, this one is his best yet! *Unlimited* captures the heart of God and clearly delineates the contested questions of our day on vital subjects such as the universal atonement. This is a rare book that challenges the scholar but is written so that a layperson will follow the discussion with ease and interest.

—**Paige Patterson**, president
Southwestern Baptist Theological Seminary

Ken Hemphill has done it again! With a passion for the gospel of Jesus Christ, Ken has pointed to the one word that describes our God—*unlimited*. These pages are worthy of study and restudy. They focus us on the remarkable nature of a God who created humans, the world, and all that is in the universe today; yet He desires a personal relationship with us!

—**Jimmy Draper**, president emeritus
LifeWay

Dr. Ken Hemphill's book *Unlimited* offers an extremely helpful, comprehendible, and thoroughly biblical resource that explains the immeasurable volume of God's divine attributes, as well as His genuine, limitless affection for every person.

—**Matt Queen**, associate professor and L.R. Scarborough Chair of Evangelism
Southwestern Baptist Theological Seminary

With brilliance and simplicity, Ken Hemphill presents the truths of an unlimited God. His observations are supported with an abundance of Scripture. I encourage you to read this uplifting and informative book.

—**Jim Richards**, executive director
Southern Baptists of Texas Convention

I have come to appreciate Ken Hemphill's gift of communicating the treasures of God's Word. *Unlimited* continues this legacy as he insightfully portrays the infinite character of God in ways that draw us into the very heartbeat of who God is. As you read, your knowledge of God will grow, your heart will be drawn into a deeper intimacy with Him, and you will be challenged to be an ambassador of God's message to a lost and needy world.

—**Larry Steven McDonald,** dean and director of DMin Studies
North Greenville University

This book is designed for small group study and is a must for every church that desires to help its members understand the extent of the atonement and become more passionate about reaching the world. I am excited that Ken has made *Unlimited* available to the local church.

—**Mac Brunson,** senior pastor
First Baptist Church of Jacksonville, Florida

Ken Hemphill brings needed clarity on the pivotal question "Who can be saved?" by demonstrating the Bible's strong affirmation that God loves every sinner everywhere and desires their salvation. A new generation of evangelicals needs to hear this word. Anyone can be saved!

—**David Hankins,** executive director
Louisiana Baptist Convention

Dr. Hemphill comes to the foundations of the Christian gospel with a heart that is pastoral, a mind that is well-trained in the Scriptures, and a pen that is passionate. *Unlimited* calls each of us to reflect on how easily we sell God short in terms of His love for His creation and His equipping of His people.

—**Gene Fant,** president
North Greenville University

Too often we are crippled in our spiritual journey because we lean too much toward our metaphysical, humanistic systems that place God in our preconceived box. In *Unlimited* Dr. Hemphill lifts the veil of understanding of God's work among the peoples of the earth. Our God authentically desires that all people everywhere come to the knowledge of being a disciple of Christ.

—**John Yeats,** executive director
Missouri Baptist Convention

UNLIMITED

God's Love,
Atonement, and Mission

KEN
HEMPHILL

FOREWORD BY MAC BRUNSON

Auxano
PRESS

Copyright © 2018 by Ken Hemphill

All Rights Reserved. No portion of this book may be reproduced in any form or by any means, electronic or print, except for brief quotations in critical reviews or articles, without the prior written permission of the publisher.

ISBN: 978-0-578-09573-8

Published by Auxano Press, Traveler's Rest, South Carolina. www.AuxanoPress.com.

Cover design: CrosslinCreative.net

Page Design and Layout: CrosslinCreative.net

Cover Image: 123RF.com

Unless otherwise noted, Scripture quotations are taken from the New American Standard Bible® (NASB), Copyright © 1960, 1962, 1963, 1968, 1971, 1972, 1973, 1975, 1977, 1995 by The Lockman Foundation. Used by permission. www.Lockman.org.

Scripture quotations marked NKJV are taken from the New King James Version®. © 1982 by Thomas Nelson. Used by permission. All Rights Reserved.

Printed in the United States of America

18 19 20 21 22 23—6 5 4 3 2 1

To
Ruby Elspeth Oswald,
my granddaughter;
a young lady who is beautiful inside and out,
loving deeply and trusting freely.
I am awed by your joy and boundless enthusiasm,
and I love watching you grow in your faith.
I am praying that you will experience and express
God's unlimited love.

CONTENTS

ACKNOWLEDGMENTS

I am grateful to the people at Auxano Press who ensure the accuracy, beauty, and serviceability of our non-disposable curricula. Josh Hunt provides countless hours behind the scene to get our materials to Bookmasters in a timely fashion. Bookmasters prints and distributes our materials. They have helped us to improve the quality and exposure of our materials. I am especially indebted to Maleah Bell who has become our project manager and primary editor. Thanks to Robin Crosslin who designs covers and interiors that make our material more attractive and readable. Our mission at Auxano Press is to provide biblically sound materials that will be used by the Holy Spirit to "cause growth" (*auxano*) in your spiritual life and in your church.

I have profited greatly from reading numerous excellent commentaries and books related to the topics and passages I have used throughout the book. Because we attempt to keep footnotes to a minimum, I have only quoted where I have directly borrowed ideas, but my debt to others who are much more skilled in the original languages is profound.

I want to personally thank David Allen, dean of the school of preaching at Southwestern Baptist Theological Seminary; David Hankins, executive director of the Louisiana Baptist Convention; and John Yeats, executive director of the Missouri Baptist Convention for their friendship and helpful suggestions as I have prepared this manuscript. I am blessed that several other friends have been kind enough to read and endorse the book while it was in process.

I am indebted to longtime friend Mac Brunson, pastor of First Baptist Church of Jacksonville, Florida, for agreeing to write a foreword. His words are gracious, and his friendship is a blessing.

Paula, my wife and ministry partner of forty-eight years, continues to be my primary sounding board. She has joyfully endured discussing the material contained in this book many times as I have struggled to make it clear and understandable in written form. Paula has a passion for the Word and the world, which is clearly reflected in all of my writing. My children and grandchildren are always in the back of my mind as I write. I want my grandchildren and their generation to love God's Word, His world, and His church with the same passion their Nana and Papa have for them. I have been dedicating my books to my grandchildren. This one is number eight in the grandkid series, and it is dedicated to Ruby Oswald.

Tina is our oldest daughter, and she and her husband Brett have three children—Lois, Micah, and Naomi. Rachael, our middle daughter, is the proud mom of Emerson, Ward, and Ruby. Katie, the youngest, is married to Daniel and they have four children—Aubrey, Sloane, Edie, and Shepherd. Our grandchildren bring us both joy and hope. It is my prayer that these books will offer them encouragement as they come to know Christ and grow to serve Him.

Finally, I want to thank Dr. Gene Fant and my colleagues at North Greenville University where "Christ makes the difference." It is my privilege to serve as special assistant to the president for denominational relations. The development of the non-disposable curricula is one facet of North Greenville's strategy to assist local churches in healthy, biblical church growth. It is our conviction that nothing changes the heart or the mind except the Word of God applied by the Spirit of God.

FOREWORD

Someone once said, "What you think about God determines everything else in life." That is a profound statement, and it is very true. When I think of God I think of so many superlatives—great, majestic, sovereign, boundless, eternal—the list could go on and on. What I do not think of, when I think of God, is "limited." All through the Word of God we are shown picture after picture of an unlimited God who loves us limitlessly.

Theologically we speak of the omnipresence of God, the omniscience of God, and the omnipotence of God. He is the living eternal Logos, without beginning and without end; in other words, He is unlimited. Personally we trust in His Word that tells us that He is a God of unlimited love, unlimited mercy, unlimited forgiveness, and unlimited grace. Never do we think of God in terms of limitations.

How could it be, with a God so limitless, that we would want to limit His greatest work, the work of Jesus Christ on the cross? Jesus stated in John 4:34, "My food is to do the will of Him who sent Me and to accomplish His work." What was the Father's will? "For this is the will of My Father, that everyone who beholds the Son and believes in Him will have eternal life, and I Myself will raise him up on the last day" (John 6:40).

There is nothing limited about the Father's will. There was nothing limited about the work of Christ. We are told in 1 John 3:8 that Jesus came to destroy the works of the devil. There is nothing in Scripture that even hints that the work of Jesus on the cross was in any way limited. He totally destroyed the works of the devil, having triumphed over sin, hell, and the grave. Neither was His atonement for sin limited. On the cross and at the tomb, Jesus was victorious and completed the will of the Father so that "whosoever will" may come.

John Calvin himself acknowledged the universal satisfaction of the work of Jesus Christ when he said:

> Our Lord Jesus bore the sins and iniquities of many. But in fact, the word "many" is often as good as equivalent to "all." And indeed our Lord Jesus was offered to all the world. For it is not speaking of three or four when it says "God so loved the world, that he spared not His only Son." But yet we must notice what the Evangelist adds in this passage: "That whosoever believes in Him shall not perish but obtain eternal life."

Ken Hemphill, with the mind of a scholar and the heart of a pastor, gives us a critical, scriptural understanding for belief in Unlimited God, including His unlimited atoning work through His Son, Jesus Christ. Ken has approached a difficult topic in a brilliant way by anchoring everything in God's character. It is not argumentative in the negative sense but a very solid way to approach the subject. I am excited that Ken has written this study. The very nature of our unlimited God, biblically and logically, declares an unlimited atonement.

Mac Brunson, senior pastor
First Baptist Church of
Jacksonville, Florida

UNLIMITED GOD

I f you have children or grandchildren you have probably watched the *Toy Story* movies. A favorite character is Buzz Lightyear whose famous line throughout the movie is "To infinity and beyond!"[1] While it is a memorable line, it is a nonsensical one. There is no possibility of going beyond "infinity." As I have attempted to write about an unlimited God, I feel a little like Buzz Lightyear in my lack of ability to speak of God who is clearly beyond our comprehension and vocabulary.

I can't remember a time when I didn't think about God. My dad was a Baptist preacher, and my earliest memories are related to church, Sunday school classes, and vacation Bible school. I memorized verses about God, talked to my parents about God, and even discussed God with my friends. I still smile when I think about my childish attempts to contemplate the nature of an unlimited or omnipotent God.

I once pondered a rather foolish idea: Could God make a rock so vast that He could not lift it? It was a childish question and one that I quickly abandoned. C. S. Lewis, the famous British scholar, asked and answered a similar question: "Can a mortal ask questions which God finds unanswerable? Quite easily, I should think. All nonsense questions are unanswerable. How many hours are there in a mile? Is yellow square or round? Probably half the questions we ask—half our great theological and metaphysical problems—are like that."[2]

In Sunday school I was taught big words that began with the prefix "omni" such as *omnipotent* or *omniscient*, and while the words expanded my vocabulary, they did little to answer my questions about an unlimited God. I still wondered how God could hear the prayers of everyone when so many people must be talking to Him at once. I shuddered to think that God knew even my unexpressed thoughts, and I wondered how He could live in heaven and yet reside in my heart. But I was most fascinated by the idea of His unlimited power.

As I continued to study, it occurred to me that God by definition was "unlimited," and any "supposed god" who was less than unlimited was no god at all. Many of the mythical gods I read about in Greek and Roman history were limited in power and were lacking in character and compassion. A deity with unlimited power but lacking in character and compassion is a frightening thought. Religions with a pantheon of deities all lack a single deity who is unlimited, and thus advocates must be sure to appease the various deities.

The affirmation of Scripture is profound in its simplicity. In preparing Israel to enter the promised land, Moses declared, "Know therefore today, and take it to your heart, that the LORD, He is God in heaven above and on the earth below; there is no other" (Deut. 4:39). The *Shema,* Israel's confession of faith, clearly reflected this conviction: "Hear, O Israel! The Lord is our God, the Lord is one! You shall love the Lord your God with all your heart and with all your soul and with all your might" (Deut. 6:4-5).

Limited Humans Discussing Unlimited God

As we begin our study about an unlimited God we must humbly acknowledge that we face serious challenges as *limited creatures* attempting to talk about an *unlimited God.* We can describe God, but we cannot fully define Him. Further, in our attempt to describe Him we must use human terms because they are the only terms we have or can understand. Therefore, a word such as *foreknowledge,* a good biblical term, is a human accommodation. Since God is not bound by time or space, nothing for Him is foreknowledge. He simply has *all knowledge.*

Isaiah the prophet expressed the human dilemma, "To whom then will you liken God? / Or what likeness will you compare with Him?" (Isa. 40:18). Simply stated, God has no equal (Isa. 40:25). Further, we must acknowledge that anything a *finite human* can know about an *infinite God* must be based on God's revelation of Himself to humanity. We are fortunate that we worship God, who has chosen to reveal Himself in creation, conscience, and human history and has provided us with a fully trustworthy record in the Bible of His self-revelation.

But herein is another challenge. Everything contained in the Bible from Genesis to Revelation bears testimony to an unlimited God. Because there is so much evidence to consider, it is difficult to limit our discussion to a few texts; and since the number of pages in this book cannot be unlimited, it will be necessary to be selective.

We will proceed by observing that throughout Scripture God's omnipotence, His unlimited power, is clearly declared. Next, we will note that God's power is evidenced in all His activity. Then, we will look at three other aspects of His omnipotence, which are expressed by the words *omniscience, omnipresence*, and *omnibenevolent*. Simply stated, the unlimited God is all-knowing, present everywhere at every time, and altogether good and giving.

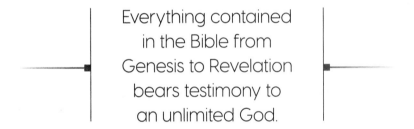

Everything contained
in the Bible from
Genesis to Revelation
bears testimony to
an unlimited God.

God's Omnipotence Declared and Evidenced in Creation

We often read the first verse of the Bible without pausing to consider the enormity of what is being declared by a seemingly simple declaration: "In the beginning God created the heavens and the earth" (Gen. 1:1). God is the subject and only actor in the first sentence of the Bible. Before anything existed there was God; He alone is self-existent. Since He existed before anything was created, the number of His years is beyond finding out (Job 36:26). All else—"the heavens and the earth"—was created by Him, thus affirming that He alone is all-powerful. The word *God* dominates the entire first chapter of the Bible and occurs thirty-five times in only thirty-one verses. God's authority as Creator has far-reaching implications.

For example, Jeremiah prophesied the captivity of Israel and then purchased a piece of "apparently" worthless land in a territory that would soon be occupied. His radical action was based on his understanding of God's omnipotence as evidenced in creation. "Ah Lord GOD! Behold, You have made the heavens and the earth by Your great power and by Your outstretched arm! Nothing is too difficult for You" (Jer. 32:17). Jeremiah's understanding of God's creative power assured him that God's promise to restore Israel would be fulfilled.

The New Testament likewise affirms that creation demonstrates God's omnipotence. John begins his Gospel with the declaration, "In the beginning was the Word, and the Word was with God, and the Word was God" (John 1:1). Hebrews 11:3 affirms that our faith is based on God's omnipotence and reliability. The author began his great chapter on faith with the affirmation that until God spoke nothing existed. "By faith we understand that the worlds were prepared by the word of God, so that what is seen was not made out of things which are visible."

God is not only responsible for all creation; He sustains it with His great power (cf. Ps. 65). Isaiah affirmed this truth in graphic language:

> Lift up your eyes on high
> And see who has created these stars,
> The One who leads forth their host by number,
> He calls them all by name;

Because of the greatness of His might and the
strength of His power,
Not one of them is missing. (Isa. 40:26)

Paul declared that God created and now sustains everything
through Christ, "for by Him all things were created, both in the
heavens and on earth, visible and invisible, whether thrones or
dominions or rulers or authorities—all things have been created
through Him and for Him. He is before all things, and in Him all
things hold together" (Col. 1:16-17). But no one expresses this
truth with greater beauty than the psalmist:

Who covers the heavens with clouds,
Who provides rain for the earth,
Who makes grass to grow on the mountains.
He gives to the beast its food,
And to the young ravens which cry. (Ps. 147:8-9)

The book of Job recounts the story of a man whose life moved
from riches to rags as he lost his wealth, his family, and his
health. As Job struggled to make sense of his circumstances, he
was forced to contemplate the reality of an omnipotent God. In
chapter 38 God addressed Job and asked him questions relating
to the creation and sustenance of everything that exists. God began, "Where were you when I laid the foundation of the earth?"
(v. 4). God then spoke of intimate details of nature and its beings,
affirming throughout that He alone has all authority. At the end
of the book, Job concluded, "I know that You can do all things, /
And that no purpose of Yours can be thwarted" (42:1-2).

Creation points to God's ultimate control of history and declares there will be an orderly conclusion. The prophet Isaiah spoke clearly of God's sovereign control of history:

> "Remember the former things long past,
> For I am God, and there is no other;
> I am God, and there is no one like Me,
> Declaring the end from the beginning,
> And from ancient times things which have not
> been done,
> Saying, 'My purpose will be established,
> And I will accomplish all My good pleasure.'"
> (Isa. 46:9-10)

God's omnipotence gives us firm assurance that everything is moving toward His ultimate purpose when He will sum up all things in Christ (Eph. 1:10).

God's Omnipotence Seen in His Activity

God's omnipotence is not only displayed in creation, it is seen in history. God called Moses to be the human instrument through which He would deliver His people from Egyptian bondage. Once Israel had passed safely through the Red Sea, they paused to sing praise to an all-powerful God:

> I will sing to the LORD, for He is highly exalted;
> The horse and its rider He has hurled into the sea.
> The LORD is my strength and song,
> And He has become my salvation;

This is my God, and I will praise Him;
My father's God, and I will extol Him. (Ex. 15:1-2)

Later in the same hymn Israel affirmed:

Who is like You among the gods, O LORD?
Who is like You, majestic in holiness,
Awesome in praises, working wonders? (v. 11)

The people of Israel were not suggesting that God is one among many gods. On the contrary, they were affirming that there is none like God. In His omnipotence He is majestic and holy, a wonder-working God. The Israelites were convinced that they had been saved through the activity of a God who is unlimited in power. He defeated all the "supposed gods" of the Egyptians as represented in the plagues. He held the pharaoh and his armies at bay and ultimately defeated them in the Red Sea.

In the book of Deuteronomy, Moses recounted the events of conquest during the wilderness wandering to prepare a new generation of Israelites to enter into the promised land. The former generation had failed to enter the land because of their lack of conviction that God had already given the land to them (cf. Num. 13–14).

According to Deuteronomy 1:21, Moses explained, "See, the LORD your God has placed the land before you." For that reason, they had no reason to fear or be dismayed. After the spies returned they reported, "It is a good land which the LORD our God is about to give us" (v. 25). Yet the people grumbled and refused to occupy the land. Moses affirmed once again, "The LORD your

God who goes before you will Himself fight on your behalf, just as He did for you in Egypt before your eyes, and in the wilderness where you saw how the LORD your God carried you, just as a man carries his son, in all the way which you have walked until you came to this place" (vv. 30-31). It was the power of an unlimited God that would make it possible for Israel to occupy the land.

The understanding that God's power is unlimited prompted David to take on the giant Goliath. Young David had journeyed to the front lines to take provisions to his brothers and to bring back good news from the battle line (1 Sam. 17:17-20). When David heard the Philistine giant hurl his arrogant challenge at the armies of the Lord, he inquired, "Who is this uncircumcised Philistine, that he should taunt the armies of the living God?" (v. 26). When Saul attempted to dissuade him, David declared, "The LORD who delivered me from the paw of the lion and from the paw of the bear, He will deliver me from the hand of this Philistine" (v. 37). When Goliath taunted David concerning his youth, he simply affirmed that he had come in the name of the Lord of hosts who would deliver the giant into his hands (vv. 45-46).

God's unlimited power is seen not only in the events of Israel; He controls the destiny of every people and nation. Daniel, who was taken captive in Babylon, was asked to recount and interpret King Nebuchadnezzar's dream. The Chaldean wise men declared that no one on earth could fulfill the desire of the king; only the gods could make known a dream and provide the interpretation (Dan. 2:10-11). Daniel asked his friends to pray that the God of heaven would give him the dream and interpretation

(vv. 17-18). Daniel's praise spoke of God's sovereignty over all nations:

> Let the name of God be blessed forever and ever,
> For wisdom and power belong to Him.
> It is He who changes the times and epochs;
> He removes kings and establishes kings;
> He gives wisdom to wise men
> And knowledge to men of understanding.
> It is He who reveals the profound and hidden
>   things;
> He knows what is in the darkness. (vv. 20-22)

Notice that Daniel spoke not only of God's control of nature but of His control of governments.

Throughout the Old Testament the writers affirm that all other "supposed" gods are but idols made by the hands of men and thus have no power of their own. As Moses was preparing the people to enter the promised land, he warned them about the dangers of living among a pagan people whose gods were man-made idols. If the Israelites acted corruptly and made an idol, they would be scattered among the people. "There you will serve gods, the work of man's hands, wood and stone, which neither see nor hear nor eat nor smell" (Deut. 4:28). The psalmist similarly declared, "For all the gods of the peoples are idols, / But the LORD made the heavens" (Ps. 96:5). Man-made idols have neither strength nor purpose and thus are not worthy of worship.

The New Testament Witness

In the New Testament, the Gospel writer Luke made it clear that the incarnation was accomplished by the unlimited power of God. When Mary asked how she could bear a son, since she was still a virgin, the angel responded, "The Holy Spirit will come upon you, and the power of the Most High will overshadow you; and for that reason the holy Child shall be called the Son of God" (Luke 1:35).

The apostle Paul declared that the cross demonstrated both the wisdom and power of God: "For the word of the cross is foolishness to those who are perishing, but to us who are being saved it is the power of God . . . but to those who are the called, both Jews and Greeks, Christ the power of God and the wisdom of God. Because the foolishness of God is wiser than men, and the weakness of God is stronger than men" (1 Cor. 1:18, 24-25; cf. Rom. 1:16). We witness the power of God at work in Christ as He taught with authority and exercised authority over demons, death, nature, and sickness. Christ's resurrection from the dead was the ultimate statement of God's unlimited power.

> Christ's resurrection from the dead was the ultimate statement of God's unlimited power.

By virtue of Christ's death and resurrection, all authority in heaven and earth was given to the exalted Lord, and that authority is the basis of the church's mission to extend His kingdom to the ends of the earth (Matt. 28:18-20).

Luke adds a significant detail to the commissioning of the disciples, "And behold, I am sending forth the promise of My Father upon you; but you are to stay in the city until you are clothed with power from on high" (Luke 24:49). In Luke's second volume he indicated that his Gospel only covers what Jesus began to do and teach (Acts 1:1). In other words, the resurrected Lord is still at work through His church. Luke focused on the promise of power in the person of the Holy Spirit, which would enable Jesus' disciples to take the gospel to the remotest part of the earth (v. 8).

Writing to the believers in proconsular Asia, Paul prayed that his readers would grasp the surpassing greatness of God's power made available to those who believe based on Jesus' resurrection (Eph. 1:19-20).

We will one day witness the unlimited power of God exercised in judgment as Satan is finally and eternally defeated. At that time, Christ will establish a new heaven and earth and abolish all death, mourning, crying, and pain. The Lord God the Almighty and the Lamb are seen as exalted on the throne (Rev. 21:1-4, 22).

Other Aspects of God's Omnipotence

Omniscience means that God knows everything. The writer of Proverbs provides a vivid picture of God's omniscience: "The eyes of the LORD are in every place, / Watching the evil and the good" (Prov. 15:3). The psalmist declares, "Great is our Lord and abundant in strength; / His understanding is infinite" (Ps. 147:5).

Daniel's conviction that God could make known to him the content and meaning of a pagan king's dream promoted him to action, which saved the life of his companions and that of the Chaldean wise men. Daniel's praise gave particular attention to God's omniscience:

> It is He who reveals the profound and hidden
> things;
> He knows what is in the darkness,
> And light dwells with Him.
> To You, O God of my fathers, I give thanks and
> praise,
> For You have given me wisdom and power;
> Even now You have made known to me what we
> requested of You,
> For You have made known to us the king's matter.
> (Dan. 2:22-23)

When Jesus taught His disciples how to practice true righteousness in regard to prayer, fasting, and the giving of alms (Matt. 6:1-18), He declared, "Your Father who sees what is done in secret will reward you" (v. 4). Our prayers should not sound like the babbling of idolaters who think they will be heard for their many words, since we pray with the certainty that our Father knows what we need before we ask Him (v. 8). God's omniscience should inform every aspect of a Christian's behavior. He is aware of our every pain, every doubt, every fear, and every triumph.

No one expresses the implications of omniscience like the psalmist in 139:1-6. His statement is not expressed in terms of sterile doctrine but in terms of adoration and praise.

God's omniscience is not like a recording device that is eternally running, recording everything without discernment. It is personal and active. In awe the psalmist declares, "Lord, You have searched me and known me" (v. 1). God knows the details of our day, our sitting down and rising up, our travels and our rest. He follows us throughout the day and watches as we lie down at night. The Lord understands our thoughts, allowing Him to know our words even before we utter them (v. 4). He surrounds us, protecting us so that He can lay His hand of blessing upon us (cf. Gen. 48:14, 17). We can affirm with the psalmist, "Such knowledge is too wonderful for me; / It is too high, I cannot attain to it" (139:6).

Some people suggest that God's omniscience means that He causes everything that occurs, whether good or bad. Such an idea is based on flawed logic rather than scriptural evidence. God is omniscient, but He is also *omnibenevolent*, which means that He is altogether good and giving. He cannot act contrary to His own character and thus cannot be the author of evil.

James wrote, "Let no one say when he is tempted, 'I am being tempted by God'; for God cannot be tempted by evil, and He Himself does not tempt anyone" (1:13). On the contrary, "Every good thing given and every perfect gift is from above, coming down from the Father of lights, with whom there is no variation or shifting shadow" (v. 17). James was affirming that God never acts contrary to His own unchanging holiness. God does not author evil to accomplish good.

Let's try an illustration that may help. Suppose you are standing on a high plateau, looking down on a raging river. Because of your location and position you can see for miles up and down the river. You notice a raft full of tourists floating lazily down the river. From your vantage point you can see they are headed for a turbulent section of the river, followed by deadly waterfalls. You begin to follow them and yell out a warning. Because they fail to heed your warning, you throw a rope to them, which they foolishly reject even as they enter the rapids. If they continue to their death, your foreknowledge of the possible consequence of their actions will not make you responsible for their deaths. The fact that God is timeless, and therefore knows everything from beginning to end, does not make Him culpable for a human's foolish choices.

The passages from James quoted above affirm the omni-benevolent aspect of God's unlimited nature. As James affirmed, He cannot do evil nor tempt others to do so, and He can only give good and perfect gifts. In Matthew 5:44-45 Jesus called on His followers to do good their enemies "so that you may be sons of your Father who is in heaven; for He causes His sun to rise on the evil and the good, and sends rain on the righteous and the unrighteous." Surely Sovereign God would not do less than He requires of His followers.

When Jesus taught His followers how to pray, He instructed them to ask, seek, and knock (Matt. 7:8). This bold approach to God in prayer is fortified by the illustration of a son asking his father for a loaf or fish and receiving the good gifts he requested. Jesus followed these examples with a simple question: "If you then, being evil, know how to give good gifts to your children, how much more will your Father who is in heaven give what is good to those who ask Him!" (v. 11).

Another important aspect of God's unlimited nature is His

omnipresence or "unlimited presence." God is present everywhere and in every moment of time. This aspect of God's unlimited power is inextricably bound to our unlimited mission, and we will devote an entire chapter to it. For a brief glimpse and classic statement of God's omnipresence, we can return once again to Psalm 139:

> Where can I go from Your Spirit?
> Or where can I flee from Your presence?
> If I ascend to heaven, You are there;
> If I make my bed in Sheol, behold, You are there."
> (vv. 7-8)

To fortify His disciples for His earthly departure, Jesus promised that He was preparing a place where they could dwell with Him eternally in His Father's house. Until that day, He would have the Father send another Helper, who would be with them forever (John 14:3, 16). One of the most unique aspects of the Christian worldview is that God is with us.

The various "omni" words used in our attempt to describe an unlimited God are vitally important and interrelated. If God were omnipotent, but not omnipresent, He would be capable of caring for us but not always able to do so because He might not be present at the time of our need. If He were omnipotent, but not omniscient, He would be unaware of our need. If He were omnipotent, but not omnibenevolent, He could be capricious like the Greek and Roman gods and thus unconcerned for our need. The God revealed in Scripture is unlimited in power, presence, knowledge, and goodness!

Limitations of an Unlimited God

As we discuss Unlimited God, we will ultimately encounter a critical question: If God is unlimited, why do evil things occur that are clearly not His purposeful will? For example, it was clearly not God's will for the Israelites to make and worship a golden calf (Ex. 32). It was not God's will for Miriam and Aaron to rebel against Moses' leadership. As a consequence, the anger of the Lord burned against them, and He removed the sign of His presence (Num. 12:9-10). God's will for the Israelites was for them to enter the promised land immediately after Joshua and Caleb assured the entire assembly that the land could be taken (13:1–14:8).

Paul declared that God's will for every believer is sanctification, which will result in abstention from sexual immorality (1 Thess. 4:3). Even though this is clearly God's will, sadly it is not fulfilled in the lives of many who are His followers. Later, in the same letter, Paul stated that God's will for believers is that we give thanks in everything (5:18). Still, like the Israelites, many of us gripe and complain continually.

An even more critical area where God's stated will is not accomplished is found in 2 Peter 3:9: "The Lord is not slow about His promise, as some count slowness, but is patient toward you, not wishing for any to perish but for all to come to repentance." Proponents of limited atonement attempt to relieve the tension created by the verse by arguing that 2 Peter 3:9 means that God is not willing for any of a certain group of persons to perish. That is special pleading, which adds an idea to this text that is clearly not present. The phrase that immediately follows, "not wishing for *any* to perish," is "for *all* to come to repentance" (my emphasis). This verse is not about a particular group of persons but about the redemption of all humanity who must repent.

God created all persons in His image and desires that none perish; yet the clear testimony of Scripture is that the gate that leads to destruction is wide, and many will enter through it (Matt. 7:13). Since God gave humans the freedom to choose, the sad reality is that "all" do not repent, and thus some do perish.

So how do we explain the *apparent* disconnect between God's "unlimited power" and the reality that His purposeful will is not always accomplished? The answer must be found in His sovereignly established self-limitation.

The only possible limitations a loving, holy, unlimited God can experience are those that He places upon Himself. Some interpreters become so tied to a system of thinking that they choose to place their own limitations on an unlimited God. However, when we look to Scripture to determine what "limits" or "boundaries" the unlimited God has placed upon Himself, we find a consistent and persistent answer. The answer is that God, in His infinite love, created humankind in His own image, meaning we are relational, rational, and thus responsible. For humans to be responsible, we must have the ability and freedom to respond to God.

The many "if—then" covenants of the Old Testament speak consistently of the necessity of human response in order to receive God's covenant promises. One of the earliest and most famous "if—then" covenants is found in Exodus 19:5-6: "Now then, if you will indeed obey My voice and keep My covenant, then you shall be My own possession among all the peoples, for all the earth is Mine; and you shall be to Me a kingdom of priests and a holy nation." The Old Testament reveals that Israel often failed to obey God's voice and keep His covenant, and they faced the consequences of their rebellion. For example, an entire generation of Israelites refused to enter the promised land under Moses, and as the consequence they wandered aimlessly in the wilderness until their deaths and failed to ever occupy the land.

God consistently affirmed to Israel that obedient response to His word would lead to blessing and that disobedience would lead to cursing (the absence of God's blessing). "See, I am setting before you today a blessing and a curse: the blessing, if you listen to the commandments of the LORD your God, which I am commanding you today; and the curse, if you do not listen to the commandments of the LORD your God, but turn aside from the way which I am commanding you today" (Deut. 11:26-28a. See also 5:29-33; 7:9-14; Josh. 1:8).

After the next generation of Israelites entered the promised land, Joshua led them in a covenant renewal ceremony. He recited Israel's history and called upon the people to "choose for yourselves today whom you will serve" (Josh. 24:15). Joshua then affirmed his own intention to serve the Lord, and the people echoed his commitment. After reminding Israel of the consequences of forsaking God, he declared that they were witnesses "that you have chosen for yourselves the LORD, to serve Him" (v. 22).

Simply put, there are consequences to the choices humans make, based on the conditions established by an unlimited God. The ability to respond to God is one aspect of what it means for man to be created in the His image (Gen. 1:26-27). It was God's will for Adam and Eve to live in perfect and eternal relationship with Him. He placed them in a beautiful garden and gave them the privilege and responsibility of tending His good creation. The only prohibition was in regard to the tree of the knowledge of good and evil. The first couple exercised their free will by choosing against God's revealed will, and the results for them and humanity were catastrophic.

Paul used the story of Adam's sin to speak about the universal rebellion of humankind. "Therefore, just as through one man sin entered into the world, and death through sin, and so death spread to all men, because all sinned" (Rom. 5:12). It is not just that Adam alone chose sin; "all" have chosen sin.

Unlimited God and the Problem of Evil

Non-Christians often raise the question of how an all-powerful God who is altogether good can allow evil and suffering. The understanding that God created man in His image with a will that allows a meaningful response explains the existence of evil in a world ruled by an unlimited, omnibenevolent God. Humanity has consistently and universally chosen to rebel. Our rebellion introduced sin into the world, and sin caused evil and death. Adam's sin brought corruption upon the entire creation. Creation itself looks forward to the eternal and final redemption of humanity, when everything will be set right again, and man will live eternally with God in a new heaven and new earth where all evil, suffering, and death will be eliminated forever (Rom. 8:18-25; Rev. 21–22).

Some people feel compelled to safeguard God's sovereignty, and they argue that God causes everything that happens. In doing so, they inadvertently make God the author of evil. For example, if God has created all people in His image, and yet has Himself determined that some of those persons, without choice, will be eternally separated from their Creator and everything good and holy, then one would have to conclude that He has caused evil.

Yet all of Scripture presents a righteous God who causes only good and not evil. James affirmed that God cannot tempt anyone to evil and He can only give good gifts (1:15-17). God's motives and actions are always pure and good. Early in Mark's Gospel, Jesus was accused of casting out demons by the power of Beelzebul (3:22). Jesus responded that Satan wouldn't cast out Satan because that would be a kingdom divided, which would ultimately lead to its demise. In the same manner, God does not do evil to accomplish good. He acts consistently based on His own character.

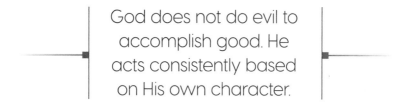

God does not do evil to accomplish good. He acts consistently based on His own character.

I once heard a lecture on the sovereignty of God in which the presenter argued that there are only two possible ways to explain the events of history and daily living: either everything happens by chance or everything occurs by the direction of Sovereign God. I remember thinking the first option is clearly unthinkable, but I was equally as uncomfortable with the second, which to me seemed to make God the author of evil. Did God actually cause Adam and Eve to sin so that He could cast them from the garden? Did He desire that Cain slay his brother? Does He desire that humans sin so that we can experience more of His grace? Paul responded to this false way of thinking in Romans 6:1-2: "Are we to continue in sin so that grace may increase? May it never be!"

I remember thinking that the lecturer's view of history actually diminished the sovereignty of God. There is a third option for viewing events in history and in our daily lives that requires a larger view of God and is consistent with the whole counsel of Scripture. Throughout the Bible we read about an adversary who is powerful but not all-powerful. He is evil by nature, and his purpose is to thwart the work of God by stealing, killing, and destroying (John 10:10). He was at work in the garden, convincing Adam and Eve that God wanted to keep them from realizing their godlike potential. He caused them to doubt the character and word of God.

A picture that came to mind that day has helped me to understand these two very different ways of viewing God's sovereign control of events. In the presenter's view God was like a chess master who was playing both sides of the boards and moving all the pieces for good or evil. We are not surprised or impressed with the chess master's ability to determine the outcome of the match when he controls all the pieces.

A view that is more consistent with the events recorded in the Bible and the events of our daily lives might be described as follows. God is the Chess Master who is playing a real adversary who is powerful but not all-powerful. The adversary can move and influence pieces on the board with the intent of defeating the Chess Master. The chess pieces in this picture can actually respond to the touch of the players. As the game progresses, it appears that the adversary has put the Chess Master in check by taking a key piece from the board—the Master's only Son. But in moving to destroy God's Son, the adversary has put himself in checkmate. The death of the Son was the ultimate defeat of Satan. Our God is truly sovereign, as demonstrated by His ability to accomplish His will despite the efforts of a real adversary and the disobedience of pieces on the chess board.

Surely this is the clear meaning of Romans 8:28-29: "And we know that God causes all things to work together for good to those who love God, to those who are called according to His purpose. For those whom He foreknew, He also predestined to become conformed to the image of His Son, so that He would be the firstborn among many brethren."

This oft quoted passage is misused frequently to suggest that God causes everything, both good and evil. "All things" may be either the subject or object of the verb phrase "work together." It is more likely the object, in which case the subject would be God. Thus, the point is that Sovereign God works in everything for the good of those who love Him and are "called according to His purpose." God can and does redeem the evil, working His good purpose through that which was intended for evil.

> Our God is truly sovereign, as demonstrated by His ability to accomplish His will despite the efforts of a real adversary.

Calling is the work of God's Spirit who convinces humans of sin and opens our eyes to the gospel, enabling us to repent and turn to Christ. In that case, we are those "who love God." God has "predestined" (predetermined) that those "who love God," to be conformed to the image of His Son. Thus, God is always at work in every circumstance, conforming us to the image of His Son. No circumstance or power can prohibit God from accomplishing His purpose in the lives of those who love Him—from the beginning of salvation, marked by His calling, to the end when He will glorify them. His sovereignty is such that He is at work in every circumstance to complete His purpose.

After promising that God is at work in everything, Paul immediately speaks of things that might happen to the believer in this life, including tribulation, distress, persecution, famine, principalities and powers (evil powers), and finally death. None of these—nothing—can separate us from the love of God. What great assurance it provides to know that God will work in every circumstance of our lives, even when we fail Him through our own disobedience, to conform us to the image of His Son until the day we are glorified (8:30, 35-39).

The account of Joseph's life in the Old Testament is an illustration of sovereign activity that cannot be thwarted by the evil choices of men, and the story consumes one fourth of the book of Genesis. Joseph was sold into slavery by his own brothers—clearly an evil action (ch. 37). He remained faithful to the Lord throughout his sojourn in Egypt and was given privilege and authority. He was ultimately made a ruler in Egypt because of his wise counsel to the pharaoh during a time of drought. Joseph's position in the government made it possible for him to provide for his extended family and thus save Israel.

When Joseph's father (Jacob) died, the brothers were afraid that Joseph would now exact revenge. When they appealed to Joseph, he first assured them they had nothing to fear: "As for you, you meant evil against me, but God meant it for good in order to bring about this present result, to preserve many people alive" (50:20). This narrative provides a great example of God working for good in everything for His people, even when humans devise evil deeds. Joseph did not overlook the evil action of his brothers that brought him to Egypt, but he recognized that God was able to bring good from it.

On September 15, 1999, during my time as president of Southwestern Baptist Theological Seminary in Fort Worth, Texas, a shooter entered the local Wedgwood Baptist Church, killing seven persons and wounding several others. Several of our seminary students were among those killed.

Soon after that terrible night, Dr. Jack McGorman, a long-time New Testament professor, was scheduled to speak in our seminary chapel service. The chapel was packed as our seminary family gathered to mourn and to be comforted. Dr. McGorman had chosen the above-mentioned text for his message. He began his message with a simple affirmation: "I must first tell you what this passage does not say. It does not say that God causes everything. He was not the one who moved the crazed shooter to take the lives of these children." He went on to explain how the adversary was at work but that God would sovereignly bring good from that which was intended for evil.

The thought of an unlimited God is a bit overwhelming to contemplate, but it is one that should cause us to seek and serve Him with all that is in us. It should lead us to worship and adore Him with our entire being. Just think—the Creator of everything knows us and loves us with a pure and absolute love. His love compelled Him to enter our world in human flesh and provide the way for dealing with our rebellion by taking upon Himself the penalty of our sin. "For God so loved the world, that He gave His only begotten Son, that whoever believes in Him shall not perish, but have eternal life" (John 3:16).

TRUTHS TO PONDER

1. Affirming that God is unlimited has profound implications. It means that He alone is the one true God, and we must respond to Him according to His revealed will and purpose. Further, it means that we must declare to everyone within our sphere of influence that they can and must know the one true God.

2. Affirming that God is unlimited also means that everything we can know about the unlimited God can only be learned from Him. We must respond to His revelation in creation, conscience, and history. His ultimate revelation is recorded in the Bible, which declares that He has fully revealed Himself in His only begotten Son, Jesus. This means we must study God's Word faithfully.

3. God has chosen to create humanity in His own image so that we understand His revelation and relate to Him in a personal way. Thus, we must respond fully to everything He

reveals to us. We study His Word for transformation and not just information. We know, so that we might obey.

4. Knowing that God is unlimited enables us to live victoriously in spite of any circumstances we might encounter daily. We can be fully assured that God is at work in everything to conform us to the image of His Son, and therefore nothing can separate us from His love.

---

1 *Toy Story*, directed by John Lasseter, (Burbank, CA: Pixar Animation Studios, 1995).

2 C. S. Lewis, "A Grief Observed," *The Complete C.S. Lewis Signature Classics* (San Francisco: HarperCollins, 2002), 460.

UNLIMITED LOVE

I n 1965 Jackie DeShannon first recorded a popular song ti-
tled, "What the World Needs Now Is Love." That sentiment
and need is still true more than fifty years later. We don't
have to look far to see that love is in great demand but short
supply. Families are struggling, churches are dividing, and our
governing officials seem always to be at odds. People have taken
to the streets with angry protests. The threat of "wars and ru-
mors of wars" seems more relevant today than ever as reports of
unspeakable war crimes are broadcast on television frequently.

In light of increasing local and global hostility and conflict,
the simple yet elegant phrase from John's Gospel—"For God so
loved the world"—seems incomprehensible. We find it challeng-
ing to love those who do not return our love; but God's love em-
braces a world in rebellion against its Creator.

The little word "so" in John 3:16 is often overlooked, but it is
critical to our understanding of the radical nature of God's love.
"So" in most English translations is an attempt to translate a

Greek word that denotes "manner" or "degree." We could translate it as "in this way" or "to such a degree." Here is an attempted
paraphrase: "God loved the world to such an amazing and unthinkable degree that He sacrificed His only begotten Son!" To
our human way of thinking, it is unimaginable that God would
give His beloved and only Son for a world that is in continuous
rebellion against Him.

The Greek word used for love in John 3:16 is *agape.* "*Agape*,
as Godlike love, stands in total contrast to all other ideas of love
in a fallen world. While they are manipulative, because largely
self-centered and working for self-interest, self-gratification and
self-protection, *agape* is completely unselfish. It is based neither
on felt need in the loving person nor on a desire called forth by
some attractive feature(s) in the one loved; it is not afraid to
make itself vulnerable, and it does not seek to get its own way by
covert ruses and psychological 'games'. It rather proceeds from
a heart of love and is directed to the other person to bless him
or her and to seek that person's highest good (cf. 1 Cor. 13:4-7).
Its source is God, and its pattern and inspiration are Jesus Christ
(1 John 4:7-9)."[1]

Love is the motive behind God's redemptive work. Love is expressed in His mercy and forgiveness. Out of God's love flows His
grace. For that reason, it is important that we attempt to understand a love that is unlimited in every dimension.

God's Love in the Old Testament

Some persons have suggested that God, as experienced throughout the Old Testament, is a God of wrath as contrasted with Jesus, the embodiment of love. Nothing could be further from the

truth. There are approximately twelve different Hebrew words used in the Old Testament to describe God's love. Among those words is *hesed*, which is so incredibly rich it is virtually untranslatable. English terms such as *lovingkindness, mercy, kindness, compassion, abiding love,* and *covenant love* are found in various Bible translations as attempts to convey the extent of God's love as expressed by the word *hesed*. When the Old Testament was translated into Greek, the Septuagint, *agape* was used more than three hundred times to refer to God's love for His people.

When attempting to understand God's unlimited love, we must remind ourselves that God is by nature unchanging or immutable—He is the same yesterday, today, and forever (Heb. 13:8). God is eternal, and thus His love is eternal, constant, and victorious over the power of evil. His eternal love, expressed and experienced by persons in the Old Testament period, is the same as the love of God experienced in and through Christ. Also, since God's essential character is holiness, His love is a *holy* love. A holy love cannot be marred by sin, nor can it tolerate sin, which is the antithesis of both holiness and love. God's holy love must judge sin, but God's love is so divinely radical that it provides an unspeakably costly solution for the sin problem that has plagued man since the garden.

The Love of God Seen in the Garden of Eden

God created humankind in His own image so that we might live in intimate relationship with Him. In chapter 1, we learned that being in God's image means that humans are relational, rational, and responsible. God provided the garden for humankind's enjoyment and care and gave them the responsibility for the stewardship of all He had created (Gen. 2:15). To further provide for the man's relational needs, He made a helper suitable for him (v. 18). In the beginning the first couple enjoyed intimate relationship with God, who is pictured as walking and talking with them in the garden (3:8). The only restriction God placed on Adam and Eve was access to the tree of the knowledge of good and evil. God's love is clearly seen in every detail of the creation and His intimate care of the humans.

> God is eternal, and thus His love is eternal, constant, and victorious over the power of evil.

In spite of God's great love and intimate care, the first couple sinned and partook of the tree of the knowledge of good and evil, which had been forbidden. Immediately their eyes were opened, and they became acutely aware of their disobedience. As a consequence, guilt and shame were first experienced by humankind. The first couple had known only good, since God is altogether good, but now they had been exposed to evil as a result of their own rebellion. Their ambition to be like God had devastating results, and shame replaced their innocence and peace. Their instinctive reaction was to hide themselves from the presence of Holy God (3:8).

In response to man's sin, the serpent was cursed, and the couple was punished and expelled from the garden. The way of reentry was barred by cherubim and a flaming sword, "which turned every direction to guard the way to the tree of life" (vv. 14-24). We should not ignore the demonstration of God's "holy" love. God's holiness required that He curse the evil one, whose purpose is to thwart all God's good plans for man, and punish man's willful rebellion. His mercy and love are clearly seen in His punishment and promises.

God had told Adam and Eve that the consequences for eating from the tree of the knowledge of good and evil would be death—that they would become mortal (2:17). As a mortal being, woman would experience pain in childbirth. For man, tending the earth would now require tedious work. The consequences of sin are seen in the ban from the garden and separation from God's immediate daily presence. The ultimate consequence of sin will be physical death as man, created from dust, returns to dust (3:16-19).

There will be enmity between the seed of the woman and the seed of the serpent, which will one day lead to the bruising of the heel of the woman's seed and ultimately crush the head of the serpent (v. 15). This verse is seen by most commentators as the first reference to the gospel where the crucifixion wounded the heel of Christ, who in His death crushed the head of the serpent.

Adam's understanding of God's promises was demonstrated by the naming of his wife "Eve," the mother of all living. The human race, though fallen, would continue through God's grace. Adam and Eve had quickly covered themselves by sewing together fig leaves (v. 7), but now God Himself clothed the couple (v. 21). Derek Kidner writes, "The coats of skins are forerunners of the many measures of welfare, both moral and physical, which man's sin makes necessary."[2]

God's holy love was demonstrated further as He barred sinful humankind from gaining access to the tree of life and thus attempting to experience immortality in a rebellious state. Man had now become like God, "knowing good and evil" (v. 22).

Before sin, humans had known only good, since God is altogether good and giving. Now they have experienced evil, and for the first time they experienced shame. By placing the cherubim to guard the entry, God protected Adam and Eve from the possibility of taking from the tree of life and living forever in a fallen state. The germ of death had infected Adam's nature as one aspect of his rebellion. God protected the couple from the tree of life because immortality apart from grace would be endless misery. It would be equivalent to what the Bible calls the second death (Rev. 2:11; 20:6, 14; 21:8).

The cherubim are seen once again as symbolic guardians of that which is holy. Later, they were carved above the ark (Ex. 37:7-9) to protect sinful people from immediate contact with that which symbolized God's holy presence. Cherubim were embroidered on the veil that barred access to the holy of holies (36:35). Only the high priest could enter, and even then only once a year, on the Day of Atonement. It is appropriate that we remind ourselves that this thick curtain that prevented access to the holy of holies was torn from top to bottom at the death of Christ (Matt. 27:51), and personal and eternal access to God was made possible through Christ's death (Heb. 10:19-22). What humankind could never gain by his own "good" accomplishments, God did through the gift of His own Son. Eternal life in the presence of Holy God was made possible for sinful persons through His unlimited, holy love.

Other Old Testament References to God's Love

The book of Genesis ends with the Israelites in Egypt. As we discussed in chapter 1, God had placed Joseph in a position of leadership in Egypt, which allowed him to provide for God's people during a time of famine. Circumstances changed quickly as a new king, who did not know Joseph, came into power (Ex. 1:8). The Israelites, once guests, were now made slaves.

God provided for their deliverance by raising up Moses to lead them out of Egypt and across the Red Sea to safety. Standing safely on dry land, Moses and the sons of Israel began to exalt the Lord through song. They affirmed,

> Who is like You among the gods, O LORD?
> Who is like You, majestic in holiness,
> Awesome in praises, working wonders? (Ex. 15:11)

The basis for God's redemptive acts? "In Your lovingkindness You have led the people whom You have redeemed; / In Your strength You have guided them to Your holy habitation" (v. 13). The word translated "lovingkindness" in this verse is the great covenant word *hesed* used in the Old Testament to describe God's unfailing love toward His people.

The giving of the Ten Commandments was based on God's lovingkindness (Ex. 20:5-6; 34:6-7). Let's look briefly at the first reference. In reading this section, you may struggle with the statement in 20:5 about God visiting the iniquity of the fathers on the third and fourth generation and miss the declaration of God's love. Notice first in verse 5 that God declared that He was "jealous" for Israel. The word *jealous* is to be understood in terms of exclusive love such as that experienced in a marriage covenant. No husband who truly loves his wife wants to share her with another man. Thus, God required that Israel not worship any idol that represented a false god (v. 4). God's love for Israel was both committed and pure.

The reference to the third and fourth generations is a typical Semitic phrase denoting continuity. It is not to be taken in an arithmetical sense. Further, it is applied to those who "hate" God and thus reject Him and refuse to live in accordance with His will as expressed in His laws.

In the last chapter we discussed God's respect of our volitional will. Since we are all interconnected, the violation of God's laws by one generation will affect generations to come. We can see this in current issues such as slavery, immorality, pollution, and drug abuse. Alan Cole writes, "What we call 'natural results' are just an expression of God's law in operation, punishing breaches of His will."[3]

Paul made a similar observation in Romans 8:18-22 concerning the ongoing consequences of sin as it impacts all of creation. "For the creation was subjected to futility, not willingly, but because of Him who subjected it, in hope that the creation itself also will be set free from its slavery to corruption into the freedom of the glory of the children of God" (vv. 20-21).

The negative aspect of the consequences of sin serves only to highlight the unlimited nature of God's love. The word translated "thousands" is used the way we would use the word *myriads* to express the limitless scope of God's love. In contrast to the consequences of humanity's rebellion is God's love that expresses lovingkindness to thousands who love Him and keep His commandments (Ex. 20:6).

After an egregious act of rebellion where the Israelites made and worshipped an idol of a golden calf, Moses smashed the tablets of the law (ch. 32). In response to Moses' prayer of intercession, God instructed him to cut out tablets like the former ones (34:1). Once again God made a declaration about His own character, which is even more expansive and would have certainly been placed in bold relief by the unspeakable rebellion of His people.

We encounter here the wonder of God's grace and the wideness of His love. "The LORD, the LORD God, compassionate and gracious, slow to anger, and abounding in lovingkindness and truth; who keeps lovingkindness for thousands, who forgives iniquity, transgression and sin; yet He will by no means leave the guilty unpunished, visiting the iniquity of fathers on the children and on the grandchildren to the third and fourth generations" (34:6-7; cf. Num. 14:18-19). God's holy love requires that He punish sin while He offers pardon to all who break His law and His heart.

> The negative aspect of the consequences of sin serves only to highlight the unlimited nature of God's love.

The book of Deuteronomy is often thought of as a book of Law because of the consistent emphasis on the demand for Israel to obey all God's laws and regulations. A rebellious generation who refused to enter the promised land had died, and Moses was preparing the next generation to enter the land.

In chapter 10 we find the account of God rewriting the tablets. In verses 12-13 Moses explained what God required of His people: "Now, Israel, what does the LORD your God require from you, but to fear the LORD your God, to walk in all His ways and love Him, and to serve the LORD your God with all your heart and with all your soul, and to keep the LORD's commandments and His statutes which I am commanding you today for your good?" Notice that God's laws are an expression of His love and that keeping them will result in "good" for all humanity. It was God who chose Israel and set His affection on them (v. 15). But God's love is not restricted to Israel. He does not show partiality. "He executes justice for the orphan and the widow, and shows His love for the alien by giving him food and clothing" (v. 18). "Alien" refers to persons not of Jewish origin.

On several occasions, pagan leaders spoke of God's love. The queen of Sheba, impressed by Solomon's wisdom, declared, "Blessed be the LORD your God who delighted in you to set you on the throne of Israel; because the LORD loved Israel forever, therefore He made you king, to do justice and righteousness" (1 Kings 10:9). Huram, king of Tyre made the same observation concerning Solomon's leadership. "Then Huram, king of Tyre, answered in a letter to Solomon: 'Because the LORD loves His people, He has made you king over them" (2 Chron. 2:11).

After the temple was constructed, the priests brought the ark into the temple while the singers praised the Lord, declaring, "He indeed is good for His lovingkindness is everlasting" (5:13). In response, God filled the house with His glory. Solomon's prayer of dedication focused on God's faithfulness and love: "O LORD, the God of Israel, there is no god like You in heaven or on earth, keeping covenant and showing lovingkindness to Your servants who walk before You with all their heart" (6:14).

When God instructed Jeremiah to write about the coming restoration of Israel, He explained that the people had found grace in the wilderness because of His love. Jeremiah wrote,

The Lord appeared to him from afar, saying,
"I have loved you with an everlasting love;
Therefore I have drawn you with lovingkindness."
(Jer. 31:3)

God told Jeremiah that there would once again be joyful singing in the streets of Jerusalem. The voices of joy and gladness will declare,

Give thanks to the Lord of hosts,
For the Lord is good,
For His lovingkindness is everlasting. (33:11)

Micah spoke of peaceful later days and the birth of a King in Bethlehem who would be from the days of eternity and shepherd His flock in the strength of the Lord (Mic. 5:2-4). What was the basis of all God's activity?

Who is a God like You, who pardons iniquity
And passes over the rebellious act of the remnant of
His possession?
He does not retain His anger forever,
Because He delights in unchanging love. (7:18)

The last prophetic word in the Old Testament begins with God declaring His love and rebellious Israel questioning it: "'I have loved you,' says the Lord. But you say, 'How have you loved us?'" (Mal. 1:2).

God's Love Fully Expressed in Christ

Jesus put flesh on the love of God. The writer of the book of Hebrews contrasted Old Testament revelation with the more complete revelation that occurred through the incarnation: "And He is the radiance of His glory and the exact representation of His nature, and upholds all things by the word of His power" (1:3a). Jesus fully and exactly embodies the nature of God, and thus His love is a perfect, holy love. This idea is clearly expressed in the Prologue of John's Gospel. John affirmed that the Word (Christ) is fully God (1:1) and thus embodies life and Light (v. 4). Further, he declared, "And the Word became flesh, and dwelt among us, and we saw His glory, glory as of the only begotten from the Father, full of grace and truth. . . . For the Law was given through Moses; grace and truth were realized through Jesus Christ" (vv. 14, 17).

Jesus put flesh on the love of God.

"Glory" refers to the manifest presence and power of God. In the Old Testament God's glory was seen as glowing fire when the Lord descended on Mount Sinai (Ex. 19:18). After the tabernacle was erected "the cloud covered the tent of meeting, and the glory of the LORD filled the tabernacle" (40:34). Later, when Solomon dedicated the temple, fire from heaven came down and consumed the sacrifices, "and the glory of the LORD filled the house" (2 Chron. 7:1). John used the term "glory" because he wanted the reader to understand that God was fully present in the person of Christ. The use of the phrase "only begotten" affirms that only Christ could fully represent God. Other messengers such as John could be sent "from" God, but only the Son could fully *express* God.

Jesus fully embodies two characteristics ascribed only to God—grace and truth. "Grace" (*charis*), is found frequently in Paul's writings, but John uses it only here in his Gospel. It is closely related to the previously mentioned Hebrew word *hesed* and could be translated as "lovingkindness" or "gracious mercy." The word translated "truth" is a major theme of John and presents the ideas of "faithfulness," "steadfastness," and "consistency."[4] Jesus alone fully embodies God's holy love, which must express both grace and truth.

Perhaps the clearest illustration of the uniqueness of holy love that manifests both grace and truth is found in John 8. The scribes and Pharisees brought a woman caught in the very act of adultery and sat her in the center of the court before Jesus. They reminded Jesus—as if He needed their counsel— of the requirement of Moses' law to stone such women. Jesus suggested that anyone without sin should be the first to throw a stone. Ironically, He was the only one qualified to bring condemnation based on the requirement to be without sin, and He refused to condemn her. One by one, the men began to file out, and Jesus asked the woman about those who would condemn her. When she indicated that no one remained, Jesus declared, "I do not condemn you, either. Go. From now on sin no more" (v. 11). Grace was expressed in forgiveness and truth in Jesus' counsel to avoid sin.

Individuals and churches struggle to balance the two. Some

churches today, in the name of grace, are soft on sin while others, in the name of truth, become legalistic. Jesus, like the Father, out of His holy love, fully embraced truth that hates sin and grace that loves the sinner.

Jesus' holy love was clearly displayed throughout His earthly ministry. When He made His first ministry appearance at the synagogue in His hometown, He declared the nature of His work by quoting from Isaiah 61:1 and 58:6.

"The Spirit of the LORD is upon Me,
Because He has anointed Me
To preach the gospel to the poor;
He has sent Me to heal the brokenhearted,
To proclaim liberty to the captives
And recovery of sight to the blind,
To set at liberty those who are oppressed;
To proclaim the acceptable year of the LORD"
(Luke 4:18-19 NKJV)

Jesus saw His ministry as one that brought good news to the world's troubled people. This list included many of the outcasts of first-century Judaism—the invisible and unlovely people. Commentators believe the words used here should be taken both literally and metaphorically. "Poor" would include not only those with little resources, but all those whose poverty means that their only hope is in God. "Liberty" may refer to healings and exorcisms for those who are physically oppressed, but it is also related to the forgiveness of sins. While Jesus healed the physically blind, the word "blind" here probably refers to all who are spiritually blind. All of humanity is "oppressed" by sin, and thus Jesus' ministry was to release those bound up in sin.[5]

At first blush the gracious words of the hometown boy were well received (Luke 4:22) until Jesus further explained the extent of His ministry. Jesus anticipated that His message and ministry would not be received well, but it was the illustrations from the ministry of the prophets Elijah, who was sent to a Gentile widow, and Elisha, who cleansed a Gentile leper, that incensed the crowd. The people were filled with such rage that they drove Jesus out of the city in an attempt to throw Him down the cliff (vv. 23-29).

This introduction to Jesus' ministry clearly indicated that His message concerning "the acceptable year of the LORD," a synonym for the good news of the "kingdom of God" (Luke 4:43), was a message for all the oppressed of the world—Jews and Gentiles alike. His message and His love were unlimited. As Jesus' ministry unfolds in the Gospels, we see unlimited love expressed to the demon-possessed, lepers, paralytics, the visually impaired, a servant of a centurion, women possessed of evil spirits and sicknesses, children, Samaritans, Gentiles, tax collectors—all sinners in need of redemption. It is not insignificant that many of Jesus' miracles were directed at Gentiles.

Jesus' calling of a tax collector to be one of His disciples was a clarion signal that God's love was available to all. While He was reclining at the table in Matthew's house, many tax collectors and sinners came and were dining with Jesus and His disciples. The Pharisees questioned the disciples about Jesus proclivity to eat with tax collectors and sinners. Jesus responded, "It is not those who are healthy who need a physician, but those who are sick. But go and learn what this means: 'I desire compassion, and not sacrifice,' for I did not come to call the righteous, but sinners" (Matt. 9:12-13).

On one particular occasion a Canaanite woman begged Jesus to heal her demon-possessed daughter (15:21-28). The disciples demanded that she be sent away. Jesus answered the disciples by affirming that He was sent to the lost sheep of the house of Israel. The woman then bowed before Jesus asking for His help. He responded by referring to the typical attitude of the Jews toward the Gentiles who considered them as little more than dogs. Undeterred, the woman humbly asked for the crumbs that would fall from the master's table. Jesus, seeing her great faith, healed her daughter. The healing demonstrated that Jesus' attitude toward the woman was in great contrast to that of the typical Jew and thus illustrates that Jesus' love was unlimited—sufficient for the Jews and Gentiles—all who hunger for wholeness.

The angst concerning Jesus' inclination to spend time with tax collectors and sinners caused the religious establishment of the day to grumble (Luke 15:1-2). In response Jesus linked together three parables of lostness—the lost sheep, the lost coin, and the lost son. A key theme of the parables is expressed in the celebration that occurs in the heavenlies when one sinner repents (vv. 7, 10).

In the parable of the lost son, the elder brother's lack of joy was a sign of his spiritual blindness that kept him from seeing his own need for repentance (v. 7). Once again we encounter the unlimited love of God, represented by the father in the final parable. He not only received the prodigal back, he went out into the field and pled with the elder brother (v. 28) to join the celebration. Jesus' love was unlimited, fully available to all who would come to Him in humble repentance.

After articulating eight woes upon those who had rejected Him and caused others to do the same, Jesus sighed, "Jerusalem, Jerusalem, who kills the prophets and stones those who are sent to her! How often I wanted to gather your children together, the way a hen gathers her chicks under her wings, and you were unwilling" (Matt. 23:37). Nothing can provide a clearer picture of the unlimited love of God, which is long-suffering, holy, pure, and unchanging. This saying occurs near the very end of Jesus' ministry, which had been consistently opposed by many of the Jewish people, particularly their religious leaders. Yet Jesus tenderly expressed His love by comparing Himself to a mother hen who desired to gather her chicks under her wings of protection. Jesus went to the cross because of His unlimited love.

God's Unlimited Love Affirmed in the Epistles

The authors of the New Testament letters theologized concerning the unlimited love of God and the redemption of humanity. Paul's letter to the Romans was intended to edify the Roman churches and to seek their help of the extension of his ministry to Spain and beyond. For that reason, Paul laid out his theological convictions in an orderly manner (chs. 1-11).

In chapter 3 he clearly established that "all," Jew and Gentile alike, have sinned and thus are in need of redemption. Paul then spoke of the death of the righteous for the unrighteous: "For while we were still helpless, at the right time Christ died for the ungodly. For one will hardly die for a righteous man; though perhaps for the good man someone would dare even to die. But God demonstrates His own love toward us, in that while we were yet sinners, Christ died for us" (5:6-8). God's unlimited love was expressed to those who were His enemies (v. 10).

Paul affirmed that it was Christ's love that caused Him to give Himself up for a sinner such as Paul (Gal. 2:20). In the Ephesian letter Paul explained that the abundance of God's mercy flowed from His great love with which he loved us. This mercy was extended to us when we were dead in our transgressions (2:4-5). Thus our redemption is a gift of God, not earned by works, but given freely by the grace of God (vv. 8-9).

We started our study of God's unlimited love in John's Gospel as we reflected on the meaning of "so loved" in John 3:16. It is beyond comprehension that God "so loved" a world in rebellion against Him that He sent His only begotten Son to die a sinner's death, so that those who believe in Him might have life. He did not send His righteous Son to judge the world that deserved condemnation, "but that the world might be saved through Him" (v. 17).

It is appropriate that we conclude this brief survey of God's unlimited love by looking at chapter 4 of John's first epistle:

> Beloved, let us love one another, for love is from God; and everyone who loves is born of God and knows God. The one who does not love does not know God, for God is love. By this the love of God was manifested in us, that God has sent His only begotten Son into the world so that we might live through Him. In this is love, not that we loved God, but that He loved us and sent His Son to be the propitiation for our sins. (vv. 7-10)

God does not simply *do* loving things; God *is* love. Thus love is the very expression of His character. The unlimited love of God was expressed by the sending of His Son into the world to be the "Savior of the world" (v. 14). His love knows no boundaries and is expressed to everyone without exception, because all, without exception, are sinners in need of God's love to be forgiven of sin and enabled to live in fellowship. God created all persons in His image to live with Him eternally and then sent His only begotten Son to redeem all of fallen humanity.

TRUTHS TO PONDER

1. God's love is eternally consistent, expressed equally in the Old and New Testaments, but made flesh through the coming of Jesus.

2. God's love is a holy love, which requires that He punish all sin but expresses itself in such measure that it provides a way for sinful humans to live eternally with a holy God.

3. His love extends to all persons and is expressed to us while we are yet ungodly and in rebellion against Him. It is His unlimited love that is the basis for His unlimited atonement.

4. Our experience with this unlimited love compels us to tell anyone and everyone that they can come to this God of love. Who do you know who needs to know of His love?

1 Sinclair B. Ferguson, David F. Wright, and J.I. Packer, eds., *New Dictionary of Theology* (Illinois: InterVarsity Press, 1988), 399.

2 Derek Kidner, *Genesis*, Tyndale Old Testament Commentaries (London: Inter-Varsity Press, 1967), 72.

3 R. Alan Cole, *Exodus*, Tyndale Old Testament Commentaries (London: Inter-Varsity Press, 1973), 156. Much of the commentary for this section follows the work of Alan Cole.

4 Gerald L. Borchert, *John 1-11*, The New American Commentary (Nashville: Broadman and Holman, 1996), 121.

5 See also Robert A. Stein, *Luke* in The New American Commentary (Nashville: Broadman and Holman, 1992), 156.

UNLIMITED ATONEMENT

When I was a child I was taught a simple little song that has stuck with me through the years. It began, "Jesus loves the little children, all the children of the world. Red, brown, yellow, black and white, they are precious in His sight." I sang the song with gusto and conviction, and its simple message impacted my life. It helped me deal with issues related to race when public schools were first being integrated. It gave me a larger view of the people of the world and their need for the gospel. The little song is certainly consistent with what we learned in the last chapter. But there are some who question whether God's atoning sacrifice includes "all the children of the world." Did Christ die only for a select group of children or did He indeed die for all of them?

The truth that God is unlimited should give us great confidence as we embrace our mission to reach the world with the gospel. Since His power is unlimited, we can be assured He provides unlimited resources and His unlimited presence, as we will see in future chapters. God's unlimited love prompted Him to send His only begotten Son as a sacrifice for our sin. Fully understanding that "God so loved the world that He gave" (John 3:16) should compel everyone who has responded to His love to take the message of His redeeming love to the entire world.

The greatest missionary of all time, the apostle Paul, declared, "For the love of Christ controls us, having concluded this, that one died for all, therefore all died; and He died for all, so that they who live might no longer live for themselves, but for Him who died and rose again on their behalf" (2 Cor. 5:14-15). The unlimited nature of God includes His provision for the salvation of all humanity.

In this chapter we will explore the extent of Christ's atonement. I have friends and colleagues who teach that the atonement is limited to a special class of persons who were marked out for salvation before they were born. Is that true, or can we confidently witness to anyone and everyone with the assurance that the death of Christ is sufficient for all, exists for all, and is efficient for all who believe?

Unlimited atonement seems to be the obvious outworking of the unlimited love of God that is clearly manifest throughout the Bible. If God created everyone out of His great love, and He desires each one to have eternal fellowship with Him, then it follows that His atonement is sufficient for all. It is hard to reconcile the idea of a *limited* atonement with God whose love is *unlimited*.

Peter affirmed that God's patience with sinful humanity was based on His desire that none perish: "The Lord is not slow about His promise, as some count slowness, but is patient toward you, not wishing for any to perish but for all to come to repentance" (2 Pet. 3:9). In writing to his young protégé, Timothy, Paul declared, "This is good and acceptable in the sight of God our Savior, who desires all men to be saved and to come to the knowledge of the truth" (1 Tim. 2:3-4).

You may have noticed in our earlier quotation from the hand of Paul the repetition of the phrase "died for all" (2 Cor. 5:14). It was not simply the love of God that compelled Paul to witness to Jew and Gentile alike, it was his assurance that Christ died "for all." Yet there are some who feel that the atonement is limited to a select group of persons, and thus we must look at the testimony of Scripture to understand what it teaches.

Defining the Atonement

There is almost universal agreement that the atonement is a central doctrine of Christianity. The word *atonement* means satisfaction or reparation for a wrong or injury. A simple definition is suggested by separating the word into its components—"at-one-ment"—which describes a state of being "at one" or being "reconciled." Thus, in Christian theology, it means the reconciliation between Holy God and sinful humans, which is accomplished through the sacrificial death of Christ. The need for atonement arises from the universal sinfulness of humankind and the total inability of fallen humanity to deal with his or her sin problem. The sin problem is not a casual matter, for the result of sin is death (Rom. 6:23). The focal point of God's atoning work is the cross where "while we were enemies we were reconciled to God through the death of His Son" (5:10).

The atonement is so magnificent that several Hebrew and Greek words are used to convey vivid word pictures related to its various aspects. As we study passages regarding the atonement, it is as if we are viewing the many brilliant colors reflected from the facets of a diamond. For example, Christ's death on the cross is viewed as having removed the curse caused by sin (Gal. 3:13); making payment of a ransom (Mark 10:45); doing away with the hostility sin caused and effecting reconciliation (2 Cor. 5:18-19); and giving an offering and sacrifice (Eph. 5:2). The picture of the sacrifice would have been a particularly vivid image to persons accustomed to offering animals on altars during worship. New Testament writers speak often of Christ's blood as the blood of sacrifice, and occasionally they refer to a particular sacrifice such as the Passover (1 Cor. 5:7), the sin offering (Rom. 8:3), or the Day of Atonement (Heb. 9:7, 11-12).[1]

Clues from the Old Testament

In chapter 2, we discussed how humankind created in God's image enjoyed unimpeded fellowship with Holy God in the garden of Eden. Sin entered the scene as both Adam and Eve violated God's word and suffered the consequences of their sin. That sin altered their relationship to God, one another, and the world in which they lived and worked (Gen. 3). Sin was not Adam's problem alone. It spread to the entire human race.

Later, in the New Testament, Paul would reflect on the result and extent of Adam's sin: "Therefore, just as through one man sin entered into the world, and death through sin, and so death spread to all men, because all sinned" (Rom. 5:12). Earlier, in Romans 3:10-18, Paul linked together numerous Old Testament references from the psalmist and the prophet Isaiah to establish the total depravity of all of humankind. The constant repetition of "none" and "not even one" underlines Paul's conclusion that all have turned aside from God's righteous standard.

Not only does the Old Testament affirm that all humanity suffers from the sin problem, it further acknowledges that humans have neither the will nor the ability to deal with it. Isaiah wrote:

> For all of us have become like one who is unclean,
> And all our righteous deeds are like a filthy
>   garment;
> And all of us wither like a leaf,
> And our iniquities, like the wind, take us away.
> There is no one who calls on Your name,
> Who arouses himself to take hold of You;
> For you have hidden Your face from us
> And have delivered us into the power of our
>   iniquities. (Isa. 64:6-7)

Paul repeated the same truth where he wrote that God, in response to humankind's rebellion, gave humankind over to the consequences of their sin (Rom. 1:28). Humans choose to sin, and God gives us the due consequences of our rebellion.

In the Old Testament, God established a process whereby humans could make offerings such as animals, incense, grain, and money to restore fellowship with God. The book of Leviticus explains the requirements and purposes of the various offerings and the role of the priests in making the sacrifices. The most significant event was the Day of Atonement when the priest entered the holy of holies to make sin offerings for himself, his family, and the assembly of Israel. After making these offerings, the nation's sins were symbolically laid on the scapegoat, which was then taken into the wilderness to die (ch. 16). The writer of Hebrews looked back to the Day of Atonement to demonstrate how Christ as the Great High Priest entered the holy place once for all through His own blood to obtain eternal redemption (9:11-14).

While the Day of Atonement was specifically established "for all the assembly of Israel" (Lev. 16:17), the very next chapter of Leviticus includes the "aliens who sojourn among them" (17:8, 10, 12-13). This phrase likely indicates what we would call a Gentile proselyte. As such those persons were subject to the Old Testament laws and regulation. The "alien who is in your town" was to be included in the hearing of the Law so that they, too, would be careful to obey it (Deut. 31:12). The atonement also extended to Gentiles.

Often Israel failed to embrace the idea that they were to be a blessing to all the nations (Gen. 12:1-3), a kingdom of priests and a holy nation "among all the peoples" (Ex. 19:5-6), but as we read the Old Testament it becomes abundantly clear that God wanted Israel to be on mission with Him in the redemption of the nations. Solomon, when dedicating the temple, spoke of the foreigner who came from a far country because of the greatness of God's name: "Then hear from heaven, from Your dwelling place, and do according to all for which the foreigner calls to You, in order that all the peoples of the earth may know Your name, and fear You as do Your people Israel" (2 Chron. 6:33).

The prophet Jonah refused to go to Nineveh because he knew

that God would forgive the sins of the Ninevites if they repented. Jonah saw the Ninevites as hated enemies of God's own people. When the reluctant prophet declared God's judgment, the people of Nineveh believed in God, and God did not bring judgment (Jonah 3:5, 10). The angry prophet remonstrated, "Please LORD, was not this what I said while I was still in my own country? Therefore in order to forestall this I fled to Tarshish, for I knew that You are a gracious and compassionate God, slow to anger and abundant in lovingkindness, and one who relents concerning calamity" (4:2). Jonah 1:9 and 4:2 demonstrate that God is Creator of all and the Redeemer of peoples apart from the elect nation of the Jews. The prophet understood that God's unlimited love would cause Him to extend salvation to the Ninevites.

Who Can Be Saved?

While the Old Testament can provide important clues about the unlimited nature of God's love, and the unlimited extent of His atonement, the New Testament is critical to our understanding of its extent since Christ Himself is the atoning sacrifice. We have already examined key texts in Jesus' ministry that demonstrated His love and ministry to the downcast and the outcast. But we must still examine passages that deal specifically with the question, who can be saved?

The words and phrases used most frequently in relationship to the matter of salvation are "whoever," "many," "as many as" "all," "everyone," and "the world." These inclusive words are used in great abundance in Scripture, and therefore we can only skim the surface in our study of God's unlimited atonement.

Whoever. The word "whoever" is found frequently in Jesus' teaching concerning the issue of response to Him. Jesus declared, "Whoever does the will of My Father" are those who are "My brother and sister and mother" (Matt. 12:50). After issuing a call to radical discipleship, He said, "For whoever wishes to save his life will lose it; but whoever loses his life for My sake will find it" (16:25). Illustrating greatness in the kingdom of heaven, He declared that people must be converted in order to enter the Kingdom. As to extent, Jesus said, "Whoever then humbles himself as this child, he is the greatest in the kingdom of heaven" (18:4). Many of these statements found in Matthew's Gospel are repeated in Mark and Luke.

In John 3:15-16, "whoever" occurs twice: "whoever believes will in Him have eternal life," and "whoever believes in Him shall not perish, but have eternal life." As Jesus was witnessing to the Samaritan woman, a despised half-breed, He said to her, "Whoever drinks of the water that I will give him shall never thirst; but the water that I will give him will become in him a well of water springing up to eternal life" (4:14). In his first letter, John affirmed this unlimited promise: "Whoever confesses that Jesus is the Son of God, God abides in him, and he in God" (1 John 4:15). In the first verse of 1 John 5, he said, "Whoever believes that Jesus is the Christ is born of God, and whoever loves the Father loves the child born of Him."

In Romans 10 Paul quoted Old Testament passages affirming "whoever believes in Him will not be disappointed," and "whoever will call on the name of the Lord will be saved" (vv. 11, 13, from Isa. 28:16 and Joel 2:32). Earlier in Romans 9:32-33, Paul spoke of the Jews who pursued righteousness through the law and not through faith, which caused them to stumble over the stumbling stone (Christ). In this instance he combined phrases from Isaiah 8:14 and 28:16 to affirm, "And he who believes in Him will not be disappointed." Notice that "whoever" (10:11, 13) and "he who" (9:33) are followed by a word that indicates a necessary response to Jesus. The entire chapter focuses on salvation being available to all who respond.

As Many As. A second important phrase is "as many as." In the parable of the marriage feast (Matt. 22:1-14) those whom the king originally invited were unwilling to come (vv. 2-3). Another invitation was issued, and some paid no attention while others abused the messengers he sent (vv. 5-6), likely a reference to the treatment of the prophets. The king commanded his servants, "Go therefore to the main highways, and *as many as* you find there, invite to the wedding feast" (v. 9, emphasis mine). The servants followed instructions and invited both evil and good (v. 10).

The invitation was clearly unlimited in scope. One of the men invited refused to wear the appropriate wedding garments, and he was cast into outer darkness (vv. 11-12). This guest was depending on his own righteousness and not appropriating the wedding clothes.

The conclusion: "For many are called, but few are chosen" (v. 14). "Many" here emphasizes the universal provision of salvation expressed clearly in the parable. "Few are chosen" indicates that while salvation is unlimited in provision, it is not universal in application. Not all will be saved, since those who rejected the invitation or refused the provision of righteousness provided by the king excluded themselves by their willful actions.

It is also likely that Matthew used the word "chosen," a

plural noun (*elektoi*) at this point as a technical term for the Jewish people who refused the original invitation and abused the messengers. In this case, the passage would also explain why so few Jews had responded to Jesus as Messiah. Either way, the parable demonstrates the unlimited invitation that requires an acceptance, and such response provides an imputed righteousness (the wedding garments).

John begins his Gospel with the affirmation that the Word, who was with God and was God, came into the world in the person of Jesus. Still, "He came to His own, and those who were His own did not receive Him. But as many as received Him, to them He gave the right to become children of God, even to those who believe in His name" (1:11-12). Once again, "as many as," is qualified by "received Him" and "believe in His name." The extent of the offer to become "children of God" is unlimited, based on an unlimited atonement, but salvation is not universal since acceptance of the offer is required.

> The extent of the offer to become "children of God" is unlimited, based on an unlimited atonement, but salvation is not universal since acceptance of the offer is required.

Two important occurrences of "as many as" are found in the book of Acts. In chapter 2, Peter had concluded the great message he delivered to a large crowd of persons from many nations on the day of Pentecost. Numerous persons who heard the message were pierced to the heart, indicating the convicting work of the Holy Spirit, and they asked Peter and the apostles what they must do. They are told that they must repent and be baptized in the name of Jesus Christ for the forgiveness of sins and the gift of the Holy Spirit. Peter then affirmed that the promise is for them, their children and for all who are far off, "as many as the Lord our God will call" (Acts 2:39 NKJV). Notice that the promise includes future generations and those "far off," a phrase from Isaiah 57:19. The reference may be to the Jews of the Diaspora or the Gentiles, emphasizing the unlimited nature of the offer of salvation. Salvation is for as many as God calls, a reference to Joel 2:32, which emphasizes the fact that God calls everyone to believe.

Those who maintain unlimited atonement fully recognize that man's response is related to God's drawing of humans to Himself. It is therefore important that we notice the linking of persons' calling upon the Lord for salvation with God's calling of them to Himself. God initiates salvation through the work of His Spirit, who convicts humans of sin, but we must respond by turning from sin and self to Christ. The limitation to atonement is not the number of persons who can be saved but the means of atonement—there is no other way to come to God except through Christ. It is Christ alone by faith alone.

A second reference in Acts is found in 13:48 when Paul was preaching in Pisidian Antioch (vv. 14-50). The events recorded in this passage help us to understand Paul's mission to the Gentiles (see verse 46). His teaching made it clear that Jews and Gentiles alike could be freed from sin through Christ and not the law. Paul's statement in verse 39 that forgiveness of sins is available through Christ to "everyone who believes" created quite a stir; and on the next Sabbath, nearly the whole city assembled to hear the word of the Lord (v. 44).

Paul's message on that second Sabbath incensed the Jews, who began to contradict him and blaspheme. He responded that it was necessary to preach to the Jews first, but their rejection of the message had proved that they were unworthy of eternal life. For this reason Paul had determined to focus on the Gentiles. He fortified his decision by quoting Isaiah 49:6, a passage that originally spoke of Israel's call to be a light to the Gentiles, which they did not fulfill.

As Messiah, Jesus fulfilled this divine destiny; and now as a messenger of the risen Christ, Paul understood that he had a mandate to be a light to the Gentiles and thus bring salvation to the ends of the earth.

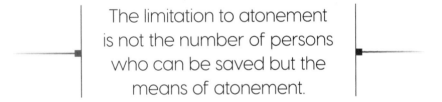

The limitation to atonement is not the number of persons who can be saved but the means of atonement.

The Gentiles responded to Paul's message with great joy "and as many as had been appointed to eternal life believed" (v. 48). The word "appointed" can also be translated as "inscribed, or "enrolled," a meaning found in papyri. Luke was likely referring to the idea that the full number of those who are to live in the coming age are already inscribed in the book of life, an idea clearly taught in Luke 10:20 and Revelation 13:8.

The overarching emphasis of the narrative is that God always intended the gospel for the Gentiles too, a point Paul made by quoting the Isaiah passage. The Gentiles responded by hearing, rejoicing, glorifying, and believing (Acts 13:48). The boundary of the gospel had been expanded to God's original intention, and the Gentiles rejoiced not because a few of them might be saved but that all who believe may be saved. A passage used by some who endorse limited atonement, when taken in the context of the entire passage in which it was placed, actually teaches the unlimited nature of the atonement to Jew and Gentile alike, which must be followed by a response initiated by the drawing of God's Spirit.

Many. The word "many" is used twice in Matthew's Gospel in reference to the atonement of Christ. Jesus said, "the Son of Man did not come to be served, but to serve, and to give His life a ransom for many" (20:28). He alone fulfilled the role of God's Servant as described in Isaiah 52:13–53:12. The phrase "to give His life a ransom for many" is one of the clearest statements of the atoning effect of Jesus' death. The Greek term translated "ransom" is used only here and in the parallel passage, Mark 10:45. However, a term built on the same Greek root is used by Paul in 1 Timothy 2:6, "who gave Himself as a ransom for *all*" (italics mine). The word translated "for" is literally "instead of," indicating that Jesus took our place and paid our ransom price.

"Many" comes directly from Isaiah 53:11 and will be repeated again in Matthew 26:28 in a context indicating Jesus' vicarious suffering. As Jesus celebrated the Passover with His disciples, He referred to His blood being poured out for forgiveness of sin, clearly echoing sacrificial language and indicating the atoning nature of His approaching death. R.T. France notes, "At Qumran and in some Rabbinic writings 'the many' is a term for the covenant community, derived probably from the use of the word in Isaiah 53:11-12 and Daniel 12:2-3,10."[2] Thus, Jesus was not restricting the extent of the atonement but was simply identifying His ministry with the Suffering Servant.

"Many" here does not contradict "all" of 1 Timothy 2:6. The Suffering Servant gave Himself as a sacrifice to create a new covenant community made up of all who trust in Him.

One of the most significant passages for the use of "many" in regard to the atonement is found in Romans 5:12-19. I would recommend that you pause and read this entire section since it is too long for a close look. For our purposes it is important that we note the alternation between "the many" and "all" throughout this section.

"Therefore," which begins the section, refers back to the affirmation that Christ died for the ungodly (v. 6), which enabled sinful humans to be reconciled to God (v. 10). Paul began by indicating the impact of the sin of the one man by which death spread "to all men, because all sinned" (v. 12). It is not simply that humans are sinners by birth; we are sinners by choice. Paul returned to this thought in verse 15, but this time he used the phrase "the many died," balancing it with the grace of God, which abounds to "the many." As in Matthew, "many" echoes Isaiah 53:11, identifying Jesus with the Suffering Servant.

Paul concluded, "So then as through one transgression there resulted condemnation to all men, even so through one act of righteousness there resulted justification of life to all men" (Rom. 5:18). Paul was affirming that Christ's death was more powerful and efficacious than was the sin of Adam and was sufficient for "all men," because it actually atoned for the sins of all people.

In Hebrews 9:23-28 the author contrasted the priesthood of Jesus with that of the Old Testament priests. Christ did not enter a holy place made by human hands, but He appeared in the presence of God to put away sin by the sacrifice of Himself. "So Christ also, having been offered once to bear the sins of many, will appear a second time for salvation without reference to sin, to those who eagerly await Him" (v. 28). The language of this section again echoes Isaiah 53:12, "He Himself bore the sin of many," and also verse 10, "He would render Himself as a guilt offering." The author anticipated Christ's reappearing when He will bring the blessings He won during His first appearance for "those who eagerly await Him." Here, again, "many" refers to all those who have responded to His sin offering and therefore eagerly await His return.

All. In Paul's letter to the Romans he frequently used the word "all" to demonstrate the sinful nature and actions of humanity and thus the universal need for atonement. In chapter 3 Paul cited numerous Old Testament passages to affirm the total depravity of humankind. He began in verse 10, "There is none righteous, not even one" and follows it in verse 12 with "All have turned aside," which echoes the thought of chapter one that indicates that humanity was given the opportunity to follow God but chose to ignore Him.

God's revelation of His character means that humans are without excuse and therefore, as verse 19 tells us, "all the world may become accountable to God." In verses 21-24 Paul affirmed that God would not make the world accountable to Him without providing a way for all humans to deal with their sinful condition: "Apart from the Law the righteousness of God has been manifested . . . "even the righteousness of God through faith in Jesus Christ for all those who believe; for there is no distinction; for all have sinned and fall short of the glory of God, being justified as a gift by His grace through the redemption which is in Christ Jesus."

In Romans 4:11 Paul referred to Abraham as the father of "all who believe." In chapter 5, a passage we looked at in our study of the word *many*, Paul declared, "So then as through one transgression there resulted condemnation to all men, even so through one act of righteousness there resulted justification of life to all men" (v. 18). In Romans 8:32, where Paul was encouraging Christians facing trials, he affirmed, "He who did not spare His own Son, but delivered Him over for us all, how will He not also with Him freely give us all things?"

Chapters 9–11 are essentially a commentary on Romans 8:28 where Paul affirmed that God is greater than evil and thus can work for good in everything. Many readers become so bogged down in a specific verse that they miss the flow of the entire section. In chapters 9 and 10 we see Paul grieving over the stubborn unbelief of his Jewish kinsmen (9:1-3; 10:21). How was it possible that the Jews had rejected their own Messiah? Paul stated in chapter 11 that Sovereign God was at work for good through the rejection of Jesus by the Jews, opening a door of salvation to the Gentiles. He further anticipated that the salvation of the Gentiles might create a jealous hunger among the Jews, thus leading to their salvation (vv. 11-12).

Throughout this entire section Paul emphasized the atonement available to "all." "For there is no distinction between Jew and Greek; for the same Lord is Lord of all, abounding in riches for all who call on Him" (10:12). The conclusion of the section is found in 11:32 and is critical for understanding the overarching theme of Romans 9–11: "For God has shut up all in disobedience so that He may show mercy to all." Notice the emphasis on "all." Paul then reflected on the riches of God's wisdom and knowledge, which are clearly beyond our comprehension (vv. 33-36). If the rejection of the Messiah by the Jews resulted in the expansion of the gospel to the Gentiles, it will ultimately bring greater glory to God as Jews and Gentiles alike respond.

Paul concluded the Roman letter with a benediction that speaks of a mystery that had been kept secret from ages past: "But now is manifested, and by the Scriptures of the prophets, according to the commandment of the eternal God, has been made known to all the nations, leading to obedience of faith; to the only wise God, through Jesus Christ, be the glory forever. Amen" (16:26-27). He spoke of this "mystery" in greater detail in Ephesians 3:1-13 and Colossians 1:25-29. The mystery included the wonderful news that the Gentiles are fellow heirs and fellow members of the body. Paul could declare confidently to the Gentiles that Christ in them was their hope of glory.

The heart of Paul's missionary enterprise is stated clearly: "We proclaim Him, admonishing every man and teaching every man with all wisdom, so that we may present every man complete in Christ" (Col. 1:28). His appeal to "every man" was based on assurance that the atonement included every person.

In Galatians, where Paul had to confront the claim of some who questioned the validity of his apostolic authority and his mission to the Gentiles, he wrote, "For you are all sons of God through faith in Christ Jesus. For all of you who were baptized into Christ have clothed yourself with Christ. There is neither Jew nor Greek, there is neither slave nor free man, there is neither male nor female; for you are all one in Christ Jesus" (3:26-28). In 2 Thessalonians Paul comforted his readers by saying, "when He comes to be glorified in His saints on that day, and to be marveled at among all who have believed—for our testimony to you was believed" (1:10).

A few additional key verses for understanding the extent of the atonement are found in 1 Timothy 2:3-6 and 4:10:

> This is good and acceptable in the sight of God our Savior, who desires all men to be saved and to come to the knowledge of the truth. For there is one God, *and* one mediator also between God and men, *the* man Christ Jesus, who gave Himself as a ransom for all, the testimony *given* at the proper time . . . For it is for this we labor and strive, because we have fixed our hope on the living God, who is the Savior of all men, especially of believers.

Paul began chapter 2 by exhorting Christians to pray "on behalf of all men," which was clearly a call for universal prayer since not all kings and men in authority were Christians. The desired result was a tranquil and quiet life exercised in godliness and dignity (vv. 1-2). Such prayer and godly lifestyle agrees with the purpose and work of "God our Savior, who desires all men to be saved and to come to the knowledge of the truth" (vv. 3-4; cf. 1:1). Paul used the passive voice of the infinitive "to be saved" rather than the active voice that would be translated "wishes to save all men," which could lead to universalism or cause some to question why He does not save everyone. God desires that all be saved, but since He gave humans free will, He does not violate our opportunity and responsibility to choose. We can pray confidently for the salvation of the lost because we are praying in accord with the heart of God.

When Paul said in verse 6 that Jesus gave Himself as a ransom for "all," it can only mean all persons without exception. Advocates of limited atonement argue that "all" means something like "some of all kinds of people"; but such is special pleading not supported by the meaning of the words, the texts themselves, or the context in which they are found.[3] Verse 6 is one of the clearest affirmations of unlimited atonement in the entire New Testament.

> God desires that all be saved, but since He gave humans free will, He does not violate our opportunity and responsibility to choose.

In 1 Timothy 4 Paul gave instructions for good servants of Christ Jesus. In verse 9 he gave the statement he would make in verse 10 greater significance by calling it a trustworthy statement that deserves full acceptance: "For it is for this we labor and strive, because we have fixed our hope on the living God, who is the Savior of all men, especially of believers" (v. 10).

There have been several suggestions as to the exact meaning of this unusual statement; however, certain truths are apparent. First, the phrase "Savior of all men" indicates that Christ was sent to be the Savior of all persons. The truth that the atonement is unlimited in its sufficiency should motivate every believer to labor and strive on behalf of the gospel. Second, the final phrase "especially of believers" indicates the necessity of personal response and rules out any idea of universalism. Third, since God is Creator of all humanity, on a temporal basis He provides blessings during the present life; but for those who believe in Him, His blessings will continue on for all eternity.

Everyone. Again we can only look at a few of the uses of "everyone" in relation to redemption. Beginning in John's Gospel, we pick up the narrative where Jesus had just said that He is the bread of life; those who come to him will not hunger, and those who believe in Him will never thirst. Jesus then stressed the Father's initiative in sending the Son and drawing people to Him (6:37).

People do not come to Christ of their own initiative; apart from the convicting and drawing work of the Spirit, humans would remain in our sin. Let's remind ourselves that John has already told us in chapter 3 that the Father loves the Son and has given "all things" into His hand (v. 35), which, in turn, leads to the affirmation in verse 36, "He who believes in the Son has eternal life; but he who does not obey the Son will not see life, but the wrath of God abides on him."

Returning now to John 6 it is important to note that the primary emphasis in this passage is on the eternal security of those who come to Christ. He will not cast them out, and He will "lose nothing, but raise it up on the last day." The assurance of eternal life is for "everyone who beholds the Son and believes in Him" (vv. 38-40).

Jesus will reiterate this truth to Martha in John 11:25-26 with the declaration, "I am the resurrection and the life; he who believes in Me will live even if he dies, and everyone who lives and believes in Me will never die. Do you believe this?" Speaking of His impending death, Jesus affirmed, "I have come as Light into the world, so that everyone who believes in Me will not remain in darkness" (12:46). The Father brings humans to Christ, but we must respond by beholding and believing in Him. Persons who believe are forever made secure by Him.

Peter, when confronted by the faith of Cornelius, affirmed that God shows no partiality and welcomes people from every nation who fear Him (Acts 10:34-35). It doesn't follow that a God who by His very character shows no partiality would make salvation available exclusively to a certain group of persons. Recounting the events of Jesus life and the commissioning of the apostles, Peter affirmed, "Of Him all the prophets bear witness that through His name everyone who believes in Him receives forgiveness of sins" (10:43).

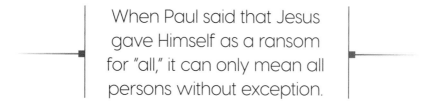

When Paul said that Jesus gave Himself as a ransom for "all," it can only mean all persons without exception.

On his first missionary journey Paul traced the activity of God from the Old Testament to Jesus. Of Him Paul said, "Therefore let it be known to you, brethren, that through Him forgiveness of sins is proclaimed to you, and through Him everyone who believes is freed from all things" (Acts 13:38-39a). Atonement is available to *everyone*, but it is effective only for the one who "fears Him," "receives Him," and "believes."

Paul, in his Roman letter, began with the statement that he was fully confident in the gospel: "For I am not ashamed of the gospel, for it is the power of God for salvation to *everyone* who believes, to the Jew first and also to the Greek" (1:16, emphasis mine). In discussing his overwhelming desire that his countrymen turn to Christ, he wrote, "For Christ is the end of the law for righteousness to everyone who believes" (10:4).

The author of Hebrews wrote, "But we do see Him who was made for a little while lower than the angels, namely Jesus, because of the suffering of death crowned with glory and honor, so that by the grace of God He might taste death for everyone" (2:9). Again, "everyone" stresses unlimited sufficiency, which becomes efficient through humanity's response.

The "World" in John's Writings

The "world" is used in numerous passages throughout the New Testament to speak of the scope of God's mission—a truth we will explore in the next chapter. But in regard to the atonement, John seems to have a unique preference for this term. Because of the frequency of John's use of the "world" in his writings, some occurrences will be mentioned without any additional commentary.

- "There was the true Light which, coming into the world, enlightens every man. He was in the world, and the world was made through Him, and the world did not know Him" (John 1:9-10).

- "The next day he saw Jesus coming to him and said, 'Behold the Lamb of God who takes away the sin of the world!'" (John 1:29).

- "For God so loved the world, that He gave His only begotten Son, that whoever believes in Him shall not perish, but have eternal life. For God did not send the Son into the world to judge the world, but that the world might be saved through Him" (John 3:16-17).

- "This is the judgment, that the Light has come into the world, and men loved the darkness rather than the Light, for their deeds were evil" (John 3:19).

- "For the bread of God is that which comes down out of heaven, and gives life to the world" (John 6:33).

- "I am the living bread that came down out of heaven; if any-one eats of this bread, he will live forever; and the bread also which I will give for the life of the world is My flesh" (John 6:51).

- "I am the Light of the world; he who follows Me will not walk in the darkness, but will have the Light of life" (John 8:12b).

- "I have come as Light into the world, so that everyone who believes in Me will not remain in darkness. If anyone hears My sayings and does not keep them, I do not judge him; for I did not come to judge the world, but to save the world. He who rejects Me and does not receive My sayings, has one who judges him; the word I spoke is what will judge him at the last day" (John 12:46-48).

- "Therefore Pilate said to Him, 'So You are a king?' Jesus answered, 'You say correctly that I am a king. For this I have been born, and for this I have come into the world, to testify to the truth. Everyone who is of the truth hears My voice'" (John 18:37).

Most of the texts listed above are self-explanatory and declare clearly God's love for and mission to the world, meaning all the people of the world. His desire is to save and not to judge, but our individual response to the Light of the World, the Lamb of God, and the bread from heaven determines whether Christ's coming will mean salvation or judgment.

Several additional texts require a brief comment. In John 16, Jesus was explaining why His departure was an advantage to the disciples. After His exaltation and ascension, He would send the Holy Spirit who would both minister to the disciples, disclosing truth to them, and would also work in the world bringing conviction of sin, righteousness, and judgment (vv. 5-15).

Verses 8-11 are the only reference to the activity of the Holy Spirit in regard to the world. In this case, the Holy Spirit acts as a prosecutor, bringing about the world's conviction. Apart from the Holy Spirit, humanity would never know the truth about sin, righteousness, or judgment. The fundamental sin is unbelief. God sent His Son into the world, and the world refused to believe. "Righteousness" is the righteousness established by the cross. The Holy Spirit alone can convince humans that we cannot depend on our own righteousness before Holy God but must accept Christ's atoning work. "Judgment" refers to Satan's defeat on the cross. Salvation, from beginning to end, is a work of God, accomplished by the Spirit, on behalf of *every* person in the whole world.

In the great High Priestly prayer from John 17, Jesus prayed first for His apostolic band: "I ask on their behalf; I do not ask on behalf of the world, but of those whom You have given Me; for they are Yours" (v. 9). His prayer for them was based on His departure from the world and their remaining in the world. He prayed that they would experience His joy, be kept from the evil one, and be sanctified in truth (vv. 11, 13, 15, 17).

Some advocates of limited atonement point to verse 9 as evidence that Jesus only prayed for the elect. They fail to notice that His prayer for His immediate disciples and those who will believe in Christ through their word is based on their mission to the world and His desire "that the world may believe that You sent Me" (vv. 18, 20-21). This passage clearly affirms God's desire that the "world" may believe, indicating the unlimited nature of the atonement.

In his first epistle John wrote, "And He Himself is the propitiation for our sins; and not for ours only, but also for those of the whole world" (1 John 2:2). There can be little question—John makes it abundantly clear that Jesus' atoning death was not only sufficient for the recipients of John's letter, but for "those of the whole world." In this letter the term "world" is often pictured as being in opposition to God, ignorant of God, under the control of the adversary, and on its way to dissolution (2:15-18; 3:1; 4:4-5; 5:19). Jesus' death is sufficient to atone for the sins of everyone in the world, but it is efficient only for "whoever believes that Jesus is the Christ" (5:1). According to verses 4-5 those born of God overcome the world by the response of their faith. "Who is the one who overcomes the world, but he who believes that Jesus is the Son of God?"

TRUTHS TO PONDER

1. The need for unlimited atonement arises from the universal sinfulness of humankind and the total inability of fallen humanity to deal with the sin problem.

2. Due to humanity's total depravity, no one seeks God. God initiates salvation and carries it to its eternal conclusion. The gospel is God's only and exclusive offer of salvation. Our response to the gospel is prompted by the convicting work of the Holy Spirit.

3. The Bible simply does not teach that atonement is limited to an elect group of persons. The suggestion that God has created a certain group of persons to spend eternity in hell with no opportunity or ability to respond to His atoning work is inconsistent with the nature of God and the witness of Scripture.

4. The New Testament utilizes words and phrases such as "whoever," "many," "as many as," "all," and "everyone" to indicate who can be saved. This means that there is no one who cannot respond to the gospel and be saved.

5. The consistent demand for a response, echoed in words such as "believe," "receive," "repent," "follow," "turn," and "reject" clearly indicates that the atonement is not universally applied nor is it unconditional. Scripture clearly teaches that even though everyone is invited to be saved, not everyone will.

6. The limitation imposed by an unlimited God is His sovereign decision to create humans as responsible, free moral agents

who must respond by faith to the singular method of salvation. Unlimited atonement avoids the extremes of universalism and determinism.

7. Understanding the extent of the atonement is not merely an academic exercise. For us to affirm that Christ died for everyone and to not seize every opportunity to present the case for Christ is inexcusable. Unlimited atonement mandates an unlimited mission.

---

1 For additional information see "Atonement" in Ferguson, Wright, and Packer, *New Dictionary of Theology*, 54-57.

2 R.T. France, *Matthew* in Tyndale New Testament Commentaries (Grand Rapids, MI: Eerdmans Publishing, 1985), 294.

3 If you are interested in going deeper and having a book that provides an extensive library of critical works on the matter, I recommend David L. Allen, *The Extent of the Atonement: A Historical and Critical Review* (Nashville: B&H Academic, 2016).

UNLIMITED MISSION

" A royal ambassador is one who represents the person of the King at the court of another." My memory of childhood events is sometimes hazy, and I may not have the exact quotation, but I can remember thinking how wonderful it was to be a Royal Ambassador. The R.A. program is an organization for boys that incorporates Scripture memory, missions awareness, and outdoor skills. While the sports and camping elements were a drawing element for most of us, I was deeply moved by the idea of being an ambassador for the King.

The Scripture verse shown on the organization's emblem is 2 Corinthians 5:20: "Therefore, we are ambassadors for Christ, as though God were making an appeal through us; we beg you on behalf of Christ, be reconciled to God." I understood that as an ambassador I had the privilege and duty to represent Christ. This verse motivated me to tell my friends about Him. But beyond that, the stories of missionaries serving around the world made me aware that there were entire people groups that had never heard the message that was so familiar to me.

The terms *missional* and *missions* have become so commonplace in the vocabulary of the average church member that they seem to mean everything and nothing at the same time. Some church members argue that everything they do is missional, while at the same time they fail to present the gospel to anyone in their own community and express little concern for those beyond their dwindling core.

Virtually every church began life with a missional intent; the desire was to extend the Kingdom by reaching the church's community and beyond. Tragically many churches quickly lose their missional focus and become introverted. This inevitably leads to stagnation and decline as members begin to focus on and argue about peripheral issues of style rather than substantive issues that impact the effectiveness of the church. Soon the church is content to survive rather than to thrive for the sake of the gospel.

Since Jesus came to establish the church, died for the church, promised to send His Spirit to fill it with power, and is coming again to receive it as His pure bride, it is appropriate that we discuss the scope of the mission He envisioned for the church. In the passage that contains the first mention of the church in the New Testament, Jesus promised that He would build His church and invest it with such authority that the "gates of Hades will not overpower it" (Matt. 16:18). After Jesus' crucifixion and mighty resurrection, He said that He had received all authority in heaven and on earth. Based on this unlimited authority He commissioned the church to "make disciples of all the nations"

(Matt. 28:18-20). In a final resurrection appearance He affirmed that the disciples would receive the power necessary to take the gospel "even to the remotest part of the earth" (Acts 1:8).

An unlimited God who expressed His unlimited love by providing unlimited atonement supplies the motivation and empowerment we need to join Him in an unlimited mission, which will one day extend to all nations and people groups of the earth. Nothing should provide greater purpose and passion for every believer and every church than the privilege of participating in the expansion of God's kingdom to every corner of the earth. While this idea is most clearly articulated in the New Testament, it is expressed clearly throughout the Old Testament as well.

Israel Selected for an Unlimited Mission

Some persons seem to think that God's concern for the nations was not expressed fully until Jesus gave the disciples the Great Commission during a resurrection appearance. Nothing could be further from the truth. God's passion from the time of the fall has been to redeem all of humanity.

The Beginning of the Story

After the fall and expulsion of Adam and Eve from the garden, sin continued unabated. God saw that wickedness was great—that every intent of man's heart was evil continually, and therefore corruption and violence filled the earth (Gen. 6:5, 11-13). Because God's justice is perfect He did not deal with sin using half measures. He acted according to His character with judgment accompanied by grace.

The phrase "all flesh had corrupted their way upon the earth" (v. 12) indicates that what God destroyed through the flood was already on the way to self-destruction by man's corruption.[1] It is not insignificant that Peter understood the judgment through the flood as a precursor of universal judgment to come at the return of the Lord (2 Pet. 3:5-7). While God cleansed the earth through the flood, He provided a means of redemption through the family of Noah, a man who walked with God (Gen. 6:9). God's holiness is revealed both in the judgment of sin and in the redemption of man.

> God's holiness is revealed both in the judgment of sin and in the redemption of man.

Once the flood subsided, and the ark was on dry ground, Noah and his family built an altar and worshipped the Lord. God gave Noah and his family the same commission He had originally given Adam and Eve—"be fruitful and multiply"— repeated three times (8:17; 9:1, 7). The whole plan of salvation had centered on one man and his family, and now that same salvation offer was to extend to the entire earth as they repopulated it. Chapters 9 and 10 tell of the expansion of Noah and his sons and the repopulation of the earth as the chosen line leads from the old world into the world of the patriarchs.

Primeval history came to a devastating climax as humans attempted to make a name for themselves with a grand project that would keep them from being scattered abroad over the face of the whole earth (11:4). Remember, humans were commissioned to multiply and fill the earth—a mission they attempted to avoid by collective disobedience. Their desire to achieve god-like status by ignoring the one true God had to be thwarted; God confused their languages and did indeed scatter them over the face of the whole earth (v. 8). The name "Babel" is the basis for the name Babylon. Babylon called itself *Bab-ili*, "gate of God," but by a play on words, Scripture imposes a truer label *balal*, "he confused." Babylon came to symbolize godless society with its persecutions (Dan. 3), pleasures, sins, superstitions (Isa. 47:8-13), riches, and eventual doom (Rev. 17–18).[2]

God's ultimate reversal of the scattering of the nations and the confusion of languages was prophesied by the prophet Zephaniah:

> "For then I will give to the peoples purified lips,
> That all of them may call on the name of the LORD,
> To serve Him should to shoulder." (3:9)

Fulfillment of this prophecy began at Pentecost, when the curse of Babel was reversed, and the gospel was understood by people of every tongue (Acts 2:5-6). The ultimate completion of reaching the nations has now been passed to our generation.

The Age of the Patriarchs

The chosen line now moves from the old world into the age of the patriarchs. According to Joshua 24:2, Terah and his forefathers "served other gods." Terah may have left Ur simply because it was destroyed in 1950 BC by the Elamites, but according to Acts 7:2-4 Abram had already heard the call of God while still living in Mesopotamia.

The history of redemption through Israel began with God speaking. Clearly He was and is the initiator of the mission to redeem all nations for His own glory. Abram, for his part, was called to forsake all and follow God's call—similar to Jesus' call to His disciples. The initiative and activity was clearly God's as the fivefold repetition of "I will" makes clear (Gen. 12:1-3). God would give Abram a land, make of him a great nation, bless him, bless those who bless him, and curse those who curse him. Those who experience God's blessing are to be a conduit of blessing to everyone they encounter. God's vision and plan was that "all the families of the earth" (v. 3) would be blessed through Abraham and his descendants.

Tragically Israel, for the most part, consumed God's blessings rather than conveyed them. The idea of a universal mission virtually disappeared from the time of the patriarchs to that of the kings with one clear exception found in Exodus 19:5-6. The concept of a missional people reappeared later in the words of the psalmist and some prophets, but it never became a program of intentional activity until the coming of Christ.

A Priestly People

The patriarchal period ended with the Israelites in Egyptian captivity. God called a reluctant Moses to lead Israel out of bondage. He fortified Moses with the assurance that He would be with him; and as a sign of His presence, He promised Moses that He would bring him back to the very same mountain where the commission was given and allow him to worship there (Ex. 3:12). We pick up the narrative in Exodus 19:4-6 where Moses descended the mountain as a spokesman for God.

God first reminded Moses that He had redeemed Israel and brought them to Himself (v. 4). God graciously chose to enter into a covenant relationship with His people. This is the first example of an "if—then" covenant, which mandates and requires a voluntary response by humans. God was not coercing Israel to serve Him the way a conquering king might have been expected to do. Further, the "if" clause described the appropriate response to One who had graciously redeemed Israel. Obedience was not a condition of deliverance but a doorway to its fullness. Their obedience was to be motivated by thankfulness for what God had already done for them. It enabled Israel to enjoy both their relationship with God and their usefulness in His redemptive plan for the earth.

As Israel responded to God in obedience, they would be His own possession, a kingdom of priests, and a holy nation (v. 6). Israel was God's by creation, and now they are uniquely His by redemption. They were His prized possession, filled with purpose and potential. Israel was now the people of God, His unique possession, designed and redeemed to carry out a crucial role in the reaching of the nations.

Walt Kaiser argues that the phrase "own possession" or "special treasure" refers to property that could be *moved* and *relocated* such as jewelry as opposed to real estate.[3] A little phrase at the end of verse 5 that is many times overlooked confirms this understanding of Israel as God's movable possession—"among all the peoples, for all the earth is Mine." God the Creator was not simply affirming His ownership of the physical earth; He was echoing His concern for all the peoples of the earth. God had not redeemed Israel to merely give them privilege and status but to give them purpose. As a movable possession, they were to be unleashed among all the peoples of the earth to reclaim them for their rightful King. They were to join God in His unlimited plan of redemption, which included "all the peoples." Like Israel, we are not simply a possession God *enjoys*, we are one He *employs*.

Perhaps you are wondering what was Israel's function as God's special, movable possession. They were to function as a holy nation and a kingdom of priests. Bear in mind that at this point in Israel's history there was no priestly class. Israel was being called to serve the one true God of the universe. They were being called to be uniquely known by their relationship with Holy God, which necessitated holy living. Their role as earthly representatives of the one true King was to extend His rightful rule to all nations. Simply stated, God desired a people who would *obey His Word, embody His name, and embrace His mission.* He still does!

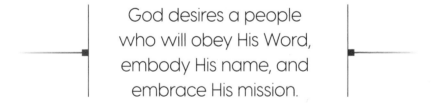

God desires a people who will obey His Word, embody His name, and embrace His mission.

You will hear a clear echo of Exodus 19 when your read 1 Peter 2:5, "You also, as living stones, are being built up as a spiritual house for a holy priesthood, to offer up spiritual sacrifices acceptable to God through Jesus Christ." Today through Christ we offer him our gifted bodies (Rom. 12:1-8); our worship

(Heb. 13:15); our service and giving (Heb. 13:15-16); and our witness (Rom. 15:16).[4]

The Construction of the Temple and a Startling Discovery

We need to press the fast-forward button and speed past the wilderness wanderings, the taking of Canaan, and the turbulent period of the judges, and stop for a moment in the early days of the monarchy. The great King David had a passionate desire to build a house of worship appropriate to the majestic Lord that Israel served—a place where the ark of the covenant, the symbol of God's presence, would dwell. David was saddened by the news that he would not be allowed to build the temple, but he was assured by God's promise that his descendant would build the house of worship. Even more important was the promise that the throne of David's lineage would be established forever (2 Sam. 7:12-16). This promise was fulfilled when Jesus, who was from the house of David, inaugurated the kingdom of God on earth.

The time of anticipation was over, and the majestic temple that Solomon built was ready for dedication. Solomon assembled the people in order: the elders, the heads of the tribes, and the leaders of the Israelite households. The priests layered themselves into position, carrying into the temple the ark of the covenant, the movable symbol of God's presence. As the ark was being placed in the temple, a cloud signifying God's presence filled the house of the Lord, and His presence was so overwhelming the priests could not continue to minister (1 Kings 8:11). While praying the prayer of dedication, Solomon was overwhelmed with God's sovereignty. He acknowledged that neither the earth nor the highest heaven could contain the Majestic One, much less this house of worship they had built (vv. 27-28).

Solomon understood that the primary purpose of the temple was for the prayer and praise of God's people. But the uniqueness of the temple cannot be fully understood unless we realize that this building was designed for more than Israel's worship needs. In truth, every blessing bestowed by God on His people is intended to have a global impact. Solomon affirmed,

> Also concerning the foreigner who is not of Your people Israel, when he comes from a far country for Your name's sake (for they will hear of Your great name and Your mighty hand, and of Your outstretched arm); when he comes and prays toward this house, hear in heaven Your dwelling place, and do according to all for which the foreigner calls to You, in order that all the peoples of the earth may know Your name, to fear You, as do Your people Israel. (vv. 41-43a)

Worship, prayer, and the reaching of the nations are all inextricably bound together. God desires to answer our prayers so that those yet to be reached will seek Him because they have witnessed His power as He has acted based on His own name.

A Couple of Prophets and a Psalmist

The desire for the foreigner to enjoy God's blessings may have been a "foreign" thought to many in Israel, but it was always God's desire. The psalmist spoke frequently of the salvation of "the peoples," "the foreigner," and "the nations." Psalm 67 provides a wonderful commentary on the idea that Israel was blessed in order that they could be a blessing to the nations. It begins,

God be gracious to us and bless us,
And cause His face to shine upon us—Selah.
That Your way may be known on the earth,
Your salvation among all nations. (vv. 1-2)

It ends with the simple declaration, "God blesses us, / That all the ends of the earth may fear Him" (v. 7). In between you will find two additional references to "nations" and five to "the peoples" or "all the peoples." God's unlimited atonement demands an unlimited mission.

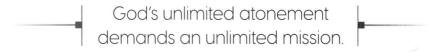

God's unlimited atonement demands an unlimited mission.

God is consumed with a love for all nations and all peoples. This is precisely why He established a royal priesthood first through Israel and now the church—to bring his message of redemption to others. The cumulative weight of Scripture speaks for itself.

All nations whom You have made shall come
and worship before You, O Lord,
And they shall glorify Your name.
For You are great and do wondrous deeds;
You alone are God. (Ps. 86:9-10)

Sing to the Lord a new song;
Sing to the Lord, all the earth.
Sing to the Lord, bless His name;

Proclaim good tidings of His salvation from day
    to day.
Tell of His glory among the nations,
His wonderful deeds among all the peoples.
    (Ps. 96:1-3)

Ascribe to the LORD, O families of the peoples,
Ascribe to the LORD glory and strength.
Ascribe to the LORD the glory of His name;
Bring an offering and come into His courts.
Worship the LORD in holy attire;
Tremble before Him, all the earth.
Say among the nations, "The LORD reigns."
    (Ps. 96:7-10a)

Praise the LORD, all nations;
Laud Him, all peoples!
For His lovingkindness is great toward us,
And the truth of the LORD is everlasting.
Praise the LORD! (Ps. 117)

Isaiah, who ministered from 740 to 701 BC, spoke often of God's concern for the nations. Prophesying in advance of Israel's liberation from captivity, he looked forward to a time when "everyone who is called by My name, and whom I have created for My glory, whom I have formed, even whom I have made" (Isa. 43:7) would know God's salvation. In chapter 49 he compared Israel to a "select arrow" created to bring Israel back to him (vv. 2, 5). Yet in a surprising twist, Isaiah declared,

"It is too small a thing that You should be My
    Servant
To raise up the tribes of Jacob and to restore the
    preserved ones of Israel;
I will also make You a light of the nations
So that my salvation may reach to the end of the
    earth." (v. 6)

Later Isaiah puts Israel's deliverance into its proper missional focus:

The LORD has bared His holy arm
In the sight of all the nations,
That all the ends of the earth may see
The salvation of our God. (52:10)

Ezekiel, the sixth century prophet, spoke during the Babylonian captivity when morale was at its lowest ebb. He declared God's intention to revive His people. God's purpose in reviving Israel had everything to do with the glory of His name and the expansion of His kingdom to the ends of the earth. God's redemptive plan for the nations would not fail, even though Israel had failed to be faithful to the covenant requiring them to be a nation of priests. God articulated first why He was prepared to act despite their disobedience: "'I will vindicate the holiness of My great name which has been profaned among the nations, which you have profaned in their midst. Then the nations will know that I am the LORD,' declares the Lord GOD, 'when I prove Myself holy among you in their sight'" (36:23).

Outside of captivity God would raise up for himself a people who would embrace His word in their hearts and not just on their lips. He would cleanse them, give them a new heart, and put His Spirit within them, enabling them to obey His word (vv. 24-27). The images that follow speak of a fruitful land with repopulated cities (vv. 33-37). Why did God desire to grant His people such abundance? "Then the nations that are left round about you will know that I, the LORD, have rebuilt the ruined places and planted that which was desolate; I, the LORD, have spoken and will do it" (v. 36). The nations have always been on the heart of God.

Zechariah, who prophesied after Israel's release from captivity, continued to call God's people to return to Him wholeheartedly. He envisioned a day of peace and prosperity, which would have an unusual but powerful effect on peoples from the nations.

> **God desires to bless us so that He might draw peoples to Himself.**

The Lord of hosts spoke to Zechariah of a day when the inhabitants of many cities would encourage one another to seek Him. People groups and mighty nations would come seeking the Lord's favor (Zech. 8:20-22). "Thus says the LORD of hosts, 'In those days ten men from all the nations will grasp the garment of a Jew, saying, "Let us go with you, for we have heard that God is with you"'" (8:23). Our relationship with the Lord should produce such total transformation that people will grab onto us because they see that God is with us. God desires to bless us so that He might draw peoples to Himself. His mission and ours are unlimited in scope.

Tragically Israel as a nation never fully understood their role of expanding God's kingdom to every nation and people group. They failed to embody His name, obey His word, and embrace His mission. When the prophets spoke of a remnant's return, they not only injected hope into deep darkness, they also projected Kingdom thinking into the future. Instead of Israel remaining the sole recipients of the covenant, there would be a righteous remnant chosen by God to reflect His name and purpose. We can rightly see the seeds of the New Testament church in this prophesied "new Israel" that would be filled with the Spirit. But that church awaited the birth of its Savior and Architect—Jesus! Through the prophet Jeremiah, God had promised that He would raise up a righteous Branch of David who would reign wisely as King and administer justice and righteousness (see Jer. 23:5-6).

The King was coming to fulfill all righteousness, to reestablish covenant continuity, and to give His righteous remnant a fresh and glorious start. While it may have seemed that David's royal line had been chopped off at the stump, there was Holy Spirit life in his family tree. Out of nowhere, a shoot was starting to grow (Isa. 11:1). He would establish a new kingdom community to whom He would give the keys of the kingdom of heaven (Matt. 16:18-19) and invest His church with such authority that they would fulfill the commission to take the message of His unlimited atonement to the nations (Matt. 28:19-20).

New Testament Teaching on the Unlimited Mission

Perhaps you were surprised that we began this chapter with an extensive look at the Old Testament. Many have concluded wrongly that God's focus on reaching all nations and all peoples began after Jesus' resurrection with the declaration we call the Great Commission (Matt. 28:19-20). Together we have seen that this is clearly not the case. God created every person in His image, and He desires that all the peoples of the earth know Him for all eternity.

The Birth, Ministry, and Teaching of Jesus

The birth of Jesus was heralded by angelic messengers, and He was visited by lowly shepherds and Persian wise men. The angelic messengers declared that His birth would bring "glory to God in the highest, / And on earth peace among men with whom He is pleased" (Luke 2:14). The peace Christ brought is universal; it encompasses all the earth and is available to all persons. Peace is made possible for everyone because God's goodwill is now clearly evidenced in the sending of His Son to be the Savior of the world.

When the prophet Simeon saw the infant Jesus, he declared,

"For my eyes have seen Your salvation,
Which You have prepared in the presence of all
    peoples,
A light of revelation to the Gentiles,
And the glory of Your people Israel." (Luke 2:30-32)

The birth of Jesus was not simply a miracle for humankind to marvel at but an act of redemption for them to appropriate and be saved. In case the obvious implication of the universal mission was missed by some, Simeon affirmed that it was for the

Gentiles, which translates the Greek *ethnos*, meaning the nations other than Israel. Since the Messiah was of the nation of Israel, His universal mission would bring glory to Israel and redemption to all peoples.

John the Baptist came preaching a baptism of repentance for the forgiveness of sins. He based His message on the words of Isaiah, which ended with the promise, "And all flesh will see the salvation of God" (Luke 3:6). "All flesh" means that all persons generally, not simply the Jews, would see God's redemption made available through Christ. Christ's mission would be unlimited in its scope. We have already looked at the beginning of Jesus' ministry in our chapter on unlimited love. We note it again at this point since the reference to the ministry of Elijah and Elisha to Gentiles clearly conveyed that Jesus' ministry would be equally as expansive. Many of the miracles Jesus performed were directed at the Gentiles who responded to Him.

On one occasion Jesus was in the synagogue on the Sabbath. To demonstrate that He was Lord of the Sabbath, He healed a man with a withered hand. The Pharisees went out and conspired to destroy Jesus. So Jesus withdrew and healed many persons privately. He warned those with Him to tell no one and then declared that these things had happened to fulfill what had been spoken through Isaiah the prophet. He identified Himself with the Beloved Servant who "shall proclaim justice to the Gentiles . . . and in His name the Gentiles will hope" (Matt. 12:18, 21).

Jesus frequently taught in parables. In Matthew 13 several parables are grouped together and often referred to as parables of the Kingdom. The focus throughout is on humankind's response to the Kingdom preaching. The response differentiates between fruitful and unfruitful soil, good grain and tares, good fish and bad, and those who find or do not find treasure. After the telling of a parable in a public setting, Jesus explained the meaning to His disciples privately so that they would understand the mysteries of the Kingdom (v. 11), contrasting them with the unresponsive crowd (v. 13).

After Jesus told the parable of the tares, His disciples asked Him for an explanation. He began by affirming that the sower was the Son of Man and that the field was the "world" (vv. 36-38). For our study, we will focus only on the extent of the sowing, which is the world, the Greek word *kosmos*. The sowing activity of Jesus, and by extension His followers, will result in the Kingdom being advanced beyond Israel to the entire world.

Late in Jesus' ministry, He spoke to His disciples about the signs that would accompany His return. One specific sign should give us great confidence as we take the gospel to the nations: "This gospel of the kingdom shall be preached in the whole world as a testimony to all the nations, and then the end will come" (Matt. 24:14; cf. Mark 13:10). Notice the twofold stress on an unlimited mission as Jesus spoke of the "whole world" and "all the nations."

While Jesus was in the home of Simon the leper, just before His final Passover, a woman poured a costly perfume over Jesus' head. While the disciples saw the act as an unnecessary extravagance, Jesus indicated that she had prepared Him for His burial. "Truly I say to you, wherever this gospel is preached in the whole world, what this woman has done will also be spoken of in memory of her" (Matt. 26:13; Mark 14:9). Here the use of the word *gospel* in a context referring to His death indicates that it is not simply Jesus' teaching that will be broadcast over the whole earth, but it is the account of His sacrificial death on behalf of all humanity. In Matthew 24:14 Jesus again mentioned the worldwide preaching of the gospel that would occur before His return.

A person's final words always have a unique impact, and that would especially be the case when the speaker had been crucified and buried and now stood alive in His resurrected body. Jesus repeated the word *all* three times in Matthew 28:18-20, beginning with "all authority." Satan had offered Jesus *all* the kingdoms of the world (Matt. 4:8-9), but now by virtue of His suffering and glorious resurrection He has received from the Father far more than Satan could offer—"all authority . . . in heaven and on earth."

Jesus' unlimited Lordship demands an unlimited mission. The disciples are to "make disciples of all the nations." "Nations" translates the regular Greek term for Gentiles. The disciples' original mission to the "house of Israel" (Matt. 10:5-6) was now expanded to include Gentiles. This in no way suggests that Jews are to be excluded. The actual Greek phrase is *panta ta ethne*, which has already been used in several contexts where Jews are included (Matt. 24:9, 14; 25:32). The mission of every disciple now includes every person and every people group.

Luke's account of the Great Commission adds several important details (Luke 24:44-49). The message must include the suffering, death, and resurrection of Jesus that made possible the forgiveness of sins. The disciples must declare the necessity of repentance for the forgiveness of sins that is proclaimed in His name. This message must be preached to "all the nations, beginning from Jerusalem" (v. 47).

The original disciples had been "witnesses of these things" (v. 48), which included Jesus ministry that fulfilled prophecy, the explanation of the Old Testament Scriptures as they bore witness to Him (v. 44), and His suffering, death, and resurrection. The message of the original witnesses, recorded in Scripture, must be the basis for every witness that comes after them. Those who bear witness need not fear that they may be inadequate for the task, because verse 49 tells us the resurrected Lord would send the promise of the Father, a clear reference to the Holy Spirit who will indwell and empower all subsequent witnesses. It is for this reason they were to wait in the city until they were "clothed with power from on high."

The Unlimited Mission in Acts and Paul's Ministry

Luke's Gospel is the story of what Jesus began to do and teach, and therefore his sequel, our book of Acts, is the story of the continuing mission of the resurrected Lord (Acts 1:1). Luke reminded the reader that Jesus had commanded the disciples to wait until they received the promise of the Father, which is now clearly identified as baptism with the Holy Spirit (vv. 4-5).

It is clear that some of Jesus' disciples were still thinking in nationalistic terms concerning the fate of Israel (v. 6). Jesus returned their focus to the promise of supernatural power and the mission to be His "witnesses both in Jerusalem, and in all Judea and Samaria, and even to the remotest part of the earth" (v. 8). The supernatural power to accomplish an unlimited mission is also unlimited, since it will be provided directly by the Holy

Spirit. We will return to the matter on unlimited resources in our next chapter.

The unlimited mission described here is an ever-expanding reach that begins in Jerusalem. This city was named first because of the work of the disciples in establishing the first Christian congregation. Jerusalem, Judea, Samaria, and the remote parts of the earth not only speak of increasing geographic reach but also increasing ethnic diversity. The Samaritans were the hated half-breeds, Jews who had married Gentiles during the time of captivity under Assyria (2 Ki. 17:24). The Gentiles were considered a despised pagan people, considered by some to be less than human. The book of Acts demonstrates the movement of the gospel to the ends of the earth: the first seven chapters cover Jerusalem; 8:1 to 11:18 covers Judea and Samaria; and the remainder traces the gospel outside the holy land until it reaches Rome.

The story of the outpouring of the Spirit at Pentecost not only speaks to supernatural empowerment, it also provides a foretaste of the unlimited mission. The disciples were filled with the Spirit and began to speak in other tongues; and "devout men from every nation under heaven" were hearing their own native languages being spoken from the mouths of the Galileans (2:5-11). Luke was speaking from his own context, and thus included languages from the Graeco-Roman world around the Mediterranean Sea. While these men were Jews, the listing of the various languages allows us to see a demonstration of the Spirit's power to communicate the gospel to those living in the uttermost parts. When we follow Paul's ministry throughout the Acts account, we see his passion for reaching the Gentiles and his unrelenting desire to go to Rome with the hope of taking the gospel to Spain.

Paul only rarely provided specific motivation in his letters to the churches to join him in the mission to the nations. This is largely related to the occasional nature of his letters to them in which he was usually addressing specific matters that had come to his attention. It is likely that he gave instructions concerning living on mission while he was present with them. We do have specific instructions for an offering to aid the church in Jerusalem during a time of famine (1 Cor. 16:1-4; 2 Cor. 8–9), which reflects earlier personal instructions. This offering would expand the ministry of the churches in Macedonia and Achaia and prove the validity of the Gentile mission (cf. Rom. 15:27).

Paul's Roman letter was written to prepare the church in Rome for his visit and to seek their assistance as he expanded the reach of the gospel to Spain (15:24). In this letter Paul spoke of his desire to preach the gospel in places where Christ had not yet been named. We would refer to these people today as "unreached people groups." He also called upon his readers to send others and to preach themselves.

In Romans 10 Paul established the unlimited nature of the atonement by citing two Old Testament passages: "For the Scripture says, 'Whoever believes in Him will not be disappointed,'" and "Whoever will call on the name of the Lord will be saved" (vv. 11, 13). At the heart of these two texts is the affirmation of the Lordship of Christ who responds to "all who call on Him" (v. 12). This truth prompted Paul to ask several missional questions: "How then will they call on Him in whom they have not believed? How will they believe in Him whom they have not heard? And how will they hear without a preacher? How will they preach unless they are sent? Just as it is written, 'How beautiful are the feet of those who bring good news of good things!'" (vv. 14-15). The church then and now must preach, send, and celebrate with those who are sent.

The End of the Story

The final chapter of the book of Acts has not been written. We are still writing our chapter in the great saga of the unlimited mission to reach the nations. However, if we glance quickly at the final book of the Bible we will be encouraged to find that the church will succeed in the reaching of the nations.

> The final chapter of the book of Acts has not been written.

In the book of Revelation the Lion from the tribe of Judah is deemed worthy to open the book with seven seals. When He takes the book the four living creatures and the elders fall down before the Lamb and sing a new song, "Worthy are You to take the book and to break its seals; for You were slain, and purchased for God with Your blood men from every tribe and tongue and people, and nation. You have made them to be a kingdom and priests to our God; and they will reign upon the earth" (5:9-10).

In John's vision of the new heaven and the new earth, he saw no temple in the New Jerusalem "for the Lord God the Almighty and the Lamb are its temple. And the city has no need of the sun or of the moon . . . for the glory of God has illumined it . . . The nations will walk by its light, and the kings of the earth will bring their glory into it . . . and they will bring the glory and the honor of the nations into it" (21:22-24, 26).

> Then he showed me a river of the water of life, clear as a crystal, coming from the throne of God and of the Lamb, in the middle of its street. On either side of the river was the tree of life, bearing twelve kinds of fruit, yielding its fruit every month; and the leaves of the tree were for the healing of the nations." (22:1-2)

Praise God, the curse of sin has been removed through the Lamb, and the people from the scattered nations will be restored to their rightful King.

TRUTHS TO PONDER

1. The unlimited mission flows from the character of Unlimited God, who expressed His unlimited love by providing unlimited atonement through the death of His Son on the cross.

2. From the time of Adam's sin until the present, God has expressed His desire that all nations and peoples be restored in relationship to their Creator and rightful King.

3. Israel was chosen and uniquely blessed so that they could in turn be a blessing to the nations, but they failed to embrace their role as a priestly people unleashed upon the world to reach the nations. Every blessing is intended to have a global impact.

4. Jesus' life, death, teaching, and ministry demonstrate that He embraced fully His Father's plan for the reaching of the

nations. He established a new covenant community—His church—made up of Jews and Gentiles in relationship with Him.

5. Paul dedicated his life to the reaching of the nations and encouraged his churches to go, send, and support mission work.

6. The book of Revelation should cause us to rejoice, because it assures us that His church will be successful in preaching the gospel to the nations and that persons from every tribe and tongue and people group and nation will join in celebration around the throne.

7. Are you and your church participating fully in the unlimited mission that is our mandate? What are you doing, and what more could you do?

---

1 An insight of Derek Kidner, *Genesis* in Tyndale Old Testament Commentaries (Downers Grove, IL; Inter-Varsity Press, 1967), 87.

2 Ibid., 110-111.

3 Walter C. Kaiser Jr., *Mission in the Old Testament* (Grand Rapids, MI: Baker, 2000), 22.

4 If you are interested in studying the missional significance in greater detail, you might enjoy my study, *EKG: The Heartbeat of God* (Nashville: Broadman and Holman, 2004). Trade books are available from Broadman and Holman; study guides, videos, and teaching guides are available from Auxanopress.com.

5

UNLIMITED RESOURCES

What would you do if you were as powerful as Superman? What would you do if you had three wishes? What would you do with a gazillion dollars? Questions such as these often introduced childhood games that called for us to imagine that we have immeasurable strength or wealth. Usually our first answers were selfish in nature, as you might imagine from young children. Then someone would come up with a serious answer such as feed the poor, and we would each, in turn, attempt to outdo our friends when it came to being generous.

As adults we can agree that it would be both childish and foolish to respond with self-interest if we were given unlimited resources. Further, it would be unthinkable to fail to appropriate and utilize such resources if they were placed at our disposal. Could it be that we are guilty of both when it comes to our spiritual resources?

Jesus' final words and grand commission to His first-century disciples was prefaced by a simple yet profound truth that clearly implied that the command to make disciples of all nations was accompanied by unlimited resources, making its completion an assured reality. "All authority has been given to Me in heaven and on earth" (Matt. 28:18b). Prior to the commission there was a declaration of authority that had to be comprehended and believed before any of these first disciples could embark upon one of the most radical missions ever conceived. *The process of restoring all the nations and peoples to their rightful King had been launched.* How could a handful of Christ followers dare to believe that they could disciple the nations? How can we?

The phrase "all authority" is based on a promise from Daniel 7:13-14 that prophetically foresaw the Son of Man being given dominion, glory, and a kingdom made up of "all the peoples, nations and men of every language." This passage had already been referenced by Jesus in His mock trial before Caiaphas the high priest (Matt. 26:57-68). Caiaphas inquired about the falsely reported boast that Jesus could destroy and rebuild the temple in three days. When Jesus remained silent, the high priest asked Jesus if He was the Christ (Messiah). In response Jesus declared that the priest had said it himself and added that soon the prophecy from Daniel concerning the Son of Man would be fulfilled: "The Son of Man sitting at the right hand of Power, and coming on the clouds of heaven" (Matt. 26:64). Jesus' bold identification of Himself with the victorious Son of Man was deemed blasphemy and was greeted by physical abuse and calls for His death.

Despite the protestation of the religious establishment, Jesus' death and resurrection affirmed His complete authority and ushered in a new era of Kingdom activity where His followers would be given unlimited resources to complete the task of making disciples of all nations. At the beginning of Jesus' ministry, Satan had tempted Him with a promise of earthly kingdoms and their glory (Matt. 4:8-10). Jesus, knowing that "all authority" would be given Him by the Father, chose to worship and serve God alone. During His earthly ministry Jesus had exercised authority over nature, disease, death, and the demonic forces; but now, by virtue of His resurrection, He has been given "all authority." It is this first "all" that leads to the repetition of "all" in the phrases "all nations," "all that I commanded," and "always."

God's unlimited love led to Jesus' death, providing an unlimited atonement, which in turn mandates an unlimited mission. His glorious resurrection and ascension assures us that unlimited resources will be provided through His unlimited presence.

The Provision of God Seen throughout the Old Testament

The Creation Story

As we open the pages of Scripture we don't have to wait long to see the theme of God's provision for humankind. The creation narrative is punctuated throughout with the assessment that everything God created was "good" (Gen. 1:4, 10, 12, 18, 21, 25), meaning that all of creation fully met God's purpose. On the sixth day God created humankind in His image, and all was deemed "very good" (v. 31). Man, the zenith of creation, was given authority over the earth and the assignment of filling and subduing the earth (vv. 26-28). Accompanying the assignment was the affirmation that God had given to humans every plant that yields seed and every tree that has fruit for food (vv. 29-30).

God created everything to provide the necessary resources for man to cooperate fully with Him in His earthly activity.

As we said in the Unlimited Love chapter, man was created in God's image as a relational, rational, and responsible being, capable of joining God in His activity on earth. God is the Creator and Owner of all that exists, and humans were His stewards, tasked with cultivating and keeping the garden God had created to supply all their needs (2:15). We see an example of delegated authority in the naming of the animals (v. 20).

All was well in the garden until the serpent convinced humankind that God's provision for them was in some way lacking, since He had prohibited them from access to the tree of the knowledge of good and evil. The first couple's sin was to doubt God's word and the total sufficiency of His provision for them.

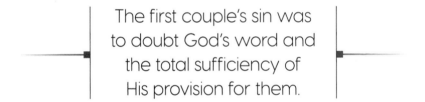

The first couple's sin was
to doubt God's word and
the total sufficiency of
His provision for them.

The Patriarchal Period

The patriarchal period began with the calling of Abram, which was accompanied with a promise of provision. We saw in chapter 4 that God promised to give Abram a land, make of him a great nation, and bless him (Gen. 12:1-3). God's blessing is His provision, presence, and protection. The abundance of God's provision is seen throughout the narrative as the land is described as a land flowing with milk and honey.

Abram's first test as he embarked on his faith pilgrimage was one that called for him to trust God's promise of provision. When God showed Abram the land of Canaan that he would soon inherit, Abram built an altar and worshipped the Lord (vv. 7-9).

Abram had barely begun his journey when he discovered that there was a famine in the land (vv. 10). His first response was to turn to Egypt for provision rather than turning to the Lord. This lack of trust led to a second sin when he lied about the identity of his wife Sarai, asking her to say she was his sister so that he would be safe and be able to secure provision in Egypt (vv. 11-13). In spite of Abram's lack of confidence in God's provision, he departed Egypt a man who was very rich in livestock, silver, and gold (13:2). God is faithful even when we are faithless.

God was patient as Abram struggled to trust fully in His provision. At various stages of Abram's journey God demonstrated His inexhaustible provision. When Abram and his nephew Lot parted ways, Lot became a prisoner of war as the result of his choice to live near Sodom. Chedorlaomer and his allies defeated the various kings that rebelled against him, which included the king of Sodom, and the victorious kings took captive Lot and all his possessions (14:12).

Abram rescued Lot, and on his return he was greeted by the king of Sodom, who offered to allow Abram to keep the spoils of war if he would return his people (v. 21). In truth, the king of Sodom had nothing to bargain with, since he had been defeated by Chedorlaomer. Abram was also met by Melchizedek, king of Salem and the priest of God Most High (*El Elyon*), who greeted him with bread and wine (v. 19). Melchizedek blessed Abram in the name of God Most High, who is declared to be the "possessor of heaven and earth." In recognition of God's abundant provision, Abram gave Melchizedek a tenth of all and refused to take anything from the hand of the king of Sodom (vv. 20, 23).[1]

A key issue in Abram's journey to rely upon God's promise to make of him a mighty nation had to do with Sarai's barren condition (Gen. 11:30). Sometime after the events in Sodom, God reiterated His promise to make Abram great. Abram answered that his only possible heir was Eliezer his servant (15:2). God asked Abram to view the vast number of stars and promised that Abram's descendants would be equally as abundant, and He promised the descendants would come through a biological child. At this juncture there appears to be a breakthrough: "Then he believed in the LORD; and He reckoned it to him as righteousness (v. 6).

The challenge to trust God continued as the years rolled by without a male heir. Sarai suggested that Abram have a child through her Egyptian maid, Hagar, and Abram did (16:1-3). Ishmael was born when Abram was eighty-six years old, but he was not to be the heir of promise.

Thirteen years later, when Abram was ninety-nine, God revealed Himself to Abram as God Almighty (El Shaddai). He repeated His promise of His abundant provision and changed Abram's name to Abraham—father of a multitude of nations (17:5) —since Abram means "exalted father," and the name was not sufficient to express the abundance of God's provision. Sarai's name was changed to Sarah, which means "mother of nations" (17:15-16).

The Lord's messengers appeared to Abraham by the oaks of

Mamre, and they reaffirmed God's promise of a biological son. When Sarah overheard the message that they would have a son, she laughed and questioned whether a woman her age could give birth to a child (18:1-2, 9-12). The messenger asked a penetrating question: "Is anything too difficult for the Lord?" He answered his own question with a bedrock promise: "At the appointed time I will return to you, at this time next year, and Sarah will have a son" (v. 14). Isaac was born at the appointed time as God had promised.

The next step in Abraham's journey to trust in God's abundant provision is told with drama unmatched in the Old Testament. God tested Abraham by commanding him to go to the land of Moriah and offer his beloved son as a burnt offering (22:1-2). Abraham's response was immediate, and he and Isaac left with two of Abraham's young men. With the mountain in view, Abraham told the young men to wait while he and Isaac went to the mountain to worship, and then they would return (v. 5).

Don't overlook the radical faith expressed by Abraham, who told the young men that that he and Isaac would return to them. The book of Hebrews tells us that Abraham dared to believe that God could raise Isaac from the dead (Heb. 11:19). His confidence in God's ability to provide was clearly maturing.

As father and son walked toward the mountain, Isaac questioned his father about the lamb for the sacrifice (Gen. 22:7). Abraham's response was profound: "God will provide for Himself the lamb for the burnt offering, my son" (v. 8a). With Isaac bound on the altar, and the knife in his hand, Abraham was interrupted by an angel. "Do not stretch out your hand against

the lad, and do nothing to him; for now I know that you fear
God, since you have not withheld your son, your only son, from
Me" (v. 12). Abraham discovered that a ram had already been
provided by God. In response, "Abraham called the name of
that place The LORD Will Provide, as it is said to this day, 'In the
mount of the LORD it will be provided'" (v. 14). This is the beautiful name *Jehovah Jireh.*

The messenger of the Lord spoke to him a second time from
heaven, affirming Abraham's absolute trust in God's provision
and reaffirming the promise of great blessing and bountiful descendants, which would enable Abraham and his descendants
to bless all the nations of the earth (vv. 15-18).

It is instructive that God's provision was fully released in
and through Abraham's life when Abraham entrusted his
most precious possession—his beloved son, the son of covenant
promise—to The LORD Will Provide. The interrelationship between God's sovereignty and man's response will always remain
a mystery to our limited understanding, but it is important to
note that God's abundant provision is related to our stewardship
of what we have already received from His hand.

The life of Joseph provides another example of God's unlimited provision. In the Unlimited God chapter we discussed
that Joseph was sold into slavery by his jealous brothers (Gen.
37). He was taken to Egypt as a captive and was made a slave
of Potiphar, an Egyptian officer. This pagan officer recognized
that the Lord was with Joseph and caused everything he did to
prosper. In response he placed Joseph over his own house, and
the Lord blessed the house of Potiphar through Joseph (39:2-6).
Joseph was later imprisoned unjustly, but the Lord again gave

him favor, and he was placed in charge of all the prisoners (vv. 19-23).

As a result of God's provision, Joseph was given a position of honor and authority, making him second only to Pharaoh (41:39-40). God gave Joseph the ability to guide Egypt through a period of seven years of famine that affected the entire area. In due time the famine impacted the Israelites, and God provided for their needs through Joseph, whom he had placed in a strategic place of leadership.

> God's abundant provision is related to our stewardship of what we have already received from His hand.

From Egypt to the Promised Land

Within a generation, the Israelites had become slaves in Egypt. God raised up Moses to lead the people from bondage. The former slaves left the land of Egypt with great abundance provided through the Egyptians because God gave the people favor in the Egyptians' sight (Ex. 12:36). The provision continued as God provided manna, quail, and water to meet the needs of a wandering people (Ex. 15–16).

The Israelites were poised to take possession of the land God had promised to give them. The spies who were sent to scout out the land all agreed that the land was bountiful, but they differed concerning Israel's ability to take it. Joshua and Caleb urged the people to enter without delay based on their confidence that the Lord would bring them into the land and give it to them (Num.

14:8-9). Tragically Israel failed to take possession of the land because of their failure to understand God's abundant provision.

Rahab—a harlot, resident of Canaan, and an unbeliever—had more confidence in God's provision than did His own people. When the next generation of Israelites returned under Joshua's leadership, she assisted the Jewish spies based on her understanding that God had already given them the land. She testified that the hearts of all the people of the land had melted away when they heard of the provision God had made for the Israelites at the Red Sea. She concluded, "For the LORD your God, He is God in heaven above and on earth beneath" (Josh. 2:11b).

After an unbelieving generation died wandering in the wilderness, Moses was preparing the Israelites to take the land under Joshua's leadership. (Much of what he taught them is found in the book of Deuteronomy.) To fortify the new generation of Israelites, Moses recited the history of God's miraculous and abundant provision to their fathers during the time of wandering. He fed Israel and assured that their clothes did not wear out nor did their feet swell from the lack of shoes during the entire time of wandering (Deut. 8:4-5).

They were now preparing to enter "a land where you will eat food without scarcity, in which you will not lack anything" (v. 9). The greatest danger they would face in this instance was a prideful attitude that would boast, "My power and the strength of my hand made me this wealth" (v. 17). Moses exhorted Israel, "But you shall remember the LORD your God, for it is He who is giving you power to make wealth, that He may confirm His covenant which He sword to your fathers, as it is this day" (v. 18).

We can clearly see several threads of emphasis coming together. Obedience to God's Word and involvement in His mission are clearly related to His unlimited provision. God desired to give Israel the power to make wealth so they could fulfill the covenant of becoming a blessing to the nations. The same is true with the church today. The temptation to think we have sufficient resources apart from God's provision leads to selfish clinging and missional failure.

Israel's Failure to Secure God's Full Provision

The theme of God's desire to abundantly supply Israel's need runs throughout the remainder of the Old Testament. For example, in the period of the Judges, Gideon was required to reduce the number of soldiers from 22,000 to 300 to demonstrate that it was God who had delivered Israel (Judg. 7:2-7).

The prophet Isaiah, prophesying Israel's return from captivity, pictured such an abundance of provision that the "sons of the desolate one will be more numerous than the sons of the married woman" (Isa. 54:1). Israel was called upon to enlarge the place of their meeting and "spare not" since they will spread abroad to the right and left (vv. 2-3). The basis of such missional confidence—"For your husband is your Maker, / Whose name is the LORD of hosts" (v. 5a).

Ezekiel pictured a time of such abundance that cities would be reinhabited, and the land would be cultivated again to such a measure that it would become like the garden of Eden (Eze. 36:33-35). The purpose and result of such abundant provision was made clear: "Then the nations that are left round about you will know that I, the LORD, have rebuilt the ruined places and planted that which was desolate; I, the Lᴏʀᴅ, have spoken and will do it" (v. 36).

Israel failed to embrace their mission to bless the nations, and thus they consumed God's provision rather than use it to bless others. We end the Old Testament narrative with the prophet Malachi who steadfastly called Israel to repent so that God's name would be great among the nations (Mal. 1:11). In spite of the spiritual apathy and outright rebellion in Israel, God spoke through the prophet and called for Israel to return to Him. They could return with confidence because God always acts in a manner consistent with His own character: "For I, the Lᴏʀᴅ, do not change; therefore you, O sons of Jacob, are not consumed" (3:6).

The specific issue of repentance concerned the lack of Israel's stewardship of all the blessings God had provided to enable them to join Him in His mission to the nations. Either out of selfish greed or lack of trust they had withheld the tithes and offerings. If they were to return to God as a missional force, they must bring the whole tithe into the storehouse. In response God promised to open "the windows of heaven and pour out for you a blessing until it overflows" (vv. 10-11). The end result—"'All the nations will call you blessed, for you shall be a delightful land,' says the Lᴏʀᴅ of hosts" (v. 12).

God always wants to provide abundant provision to those who join Him in His mission. He has chosen to work in cooperation with humankind, making His provision available through our obedient response to His Word and His mission. Tragically Israel ignored God's call to repentance through Malachi, and four hundred years of silence followed.

God's Unlimited Provision in the New Testament

In the New Testament we see Jesus as both the recipient and dispenser of God's abundant provision. Jesus readily declared His absolute dependence upon His Father, declaring, "Truly, truly, I say to you, the Son can do nothing of Himself, unless it is something He sees the Father doing; for whatever the Father does, these things the Son also does in like manner" (John 5:19). Just after the Passover meal with His disciples, Jesus again said, "Do you not believe that I am in the Father, and the Father is in Me? The words that I say to you I do not speak on My own initiative, but the Father abiding in Me does His works" (John 14:10).

Jesus' authority was expressed in His teaching. It was clearly evident as He dealt with disease, the demonic, and nature itself.

Evidenced in the Ministry of Jesus

Matthew begins his account of Jesus' adult life with His baptism by John, followed immediately by the temptation in the wilderness (3:13–4:11). The devil first tempted Jesus by physical hunger, and Jesus responded based on Deuteronomy 8:3, affirming that man lives on every word proceeding from the mouth of the Father. The devil then took Jesus to the pinnacle of the temple and tempted Him to hurl Himself down so that the angels would come to His aid. Once again, Jesus responded from Deuteronomy (6:16), stating that man should not put God to the test. In the final temptation, the devil offered Jesus "all the kingdoms of the world and their glory" (Matt. 4:8). Jesus rebuked Satan, quoting Deuteronomy 6:13, and declaring His commitment to worship God alone.

Time and again, Israel had failed to trust in God's provision that was available to enable them to bless the nations. Jesus, however, determined to accomplish His mission by God's provision alone.

A seminal illustration of the abundance of resources made available to and through Jesus is found in the feeding of the five thousand. Seeing the large crowd, Jesus asked Philip where they could buy enough bread to feed everyone. John's Gospel tells us that Jesus was testing Philip, "for He Himself knew what He was intending to do" (6:6). Philip began calculating the cost of such a colossal undertaking. His math failed to take into account God's unlimited provision made available through His Son.

When Andrew discovered a lad with five barley loaves and two fish, Jesus had the people sit down. After Jesus gave thanks He distributed to the seated multitude "as much as they wanted" (v. 11). This was not a snack to hold them over until they could return home but a fully satisfying meal. God's provision is more than sufficient, and thus the disciples gathered up twelve baskets with leftover fragments.

Promised to His Disciples

Jesus not only depended upon God's abundant provision, but He taught His disciples to do the same. In Matthew's account, which begins with the Sermon on the Mount, Jesus taught His disciples to pray (Matt. 6:1-15). He warned them against meaningless repetition as practiced by the Gentiles (pagans) who were uncertain as to whether any deity was hearing and responding. The reason the disciples could have confidence as they prayed— "Your Father knows what you need before you ask Him" (v. 8).

The disciples were told to pray for daily bread, forgiveness of debts, and for deliverance from evil (vv. 11-13). Daily bread would have certainly reminded them of the daily manna provided during the Israelites' wilderness wanderings. God's provision is daily and sufficient. The forgiveness of sins is so overwhelmingly abundant that it enables us to forgive those who have sinned against us. His deliverance from evil is based on His nature, which is wholly righteous.

It is important to note that abundant Kingdom provision is related to the commitment to be on mission with God. The first three statements of the prayer—"Hallowed be Your name," "Your kingdom come," and "Your will be done"—are our commitments to God. We are not giving God permission for His name to be holy; we are asking Him to make His name holy in our lives. We are not giving Him permission for His kingdom to come; we are asking Him to show us His kingdom activity and allow us to join Him in His work. We are pledging immediate and complete obedience. God's unlimited provision is provided to enable us to complete His kingdom work on earth until we join Him in heaven.

Jesus' instruction on prayer is followed by the warning in verse 19 about storing up treasure on earth that is transient, not eternal. Earthly treasure has no value if it does not promote Kingdom activity and can become a stumbling block to those who are called to be on mission with Him. Earthly treasure, without Kingdom focus, can cause anxiety and keep a person from effective Kingdom activity.

The terms "worry" or "worried" are repeated five times in verses 25-34 on matters related to provision for one's life—food, drink, clothing, an extra hour of time, and tomorrow. Jesus concluded by affirming that Gentiles experience these same needs without the confidence that they have a heavenly Father who knows their need of such necessities (v. 32). Kingdom focus is the antidote for worry: "But seek first His kingdom and His righteousness, and all these things will be added to you" (v. 33). God's provision defeats worry and enables us to fully participate in His kingdom activity.[2]

Earthly treasure, without Kingdom focus, can cause anxiety and keep a person from effective Kingdom activity.

After Jesus took the Passover meal with His disciples, He spoke candidly of His impending betrayal and death. The disciples were confused and frightened by the news. After He comforted them with the assurance of an ultimate dwelling with Him in His Father's house, He challenged them with an astounding truth: "Truly, truly, I say to you, he who believes in Me, the works that I do, he will do also; and greater works than these he will do; because I go to the Father" (John 14:12).

Jesus' departure opened an entirely new avenue of provision for disciples of every generation. His earthly ministry had been empowered by the Father abiding in Jesus (v. 10), and now the followers of Jesus would have constant access to the full resources of God as the Holy Spirit came to abide in them. Jesus had been their earthly Helper through the incarnation, but now there would be "another Helper" who would be with them forever. They would not be helpless and destitute like orphans (v. 18). Empowered by the Spirit, they would bear much fruit that would remain (15:16).

The Helper would teach them and quicken their memory (14:26); He would testify about Jesus (15:26); He would convict the world of sin, righteousness, and judgment (16:8-11); and He would guide the disciples into all truth and disclose the things of the Father to them (16:13-15). While space will not allow us to comment on every verse in this section, it is crystal clear that God's provision, which had been seen clearly in Jesus' ministry, has been made accessible to every believer by the indwelling presence and empowering of the Holy Spirit.

Before we leave this section, it is important that we take a glimpse at Jesus' final prayer for His disciples. He prayed for them specifically because He was now sending them into the world with the very mission the Father had given Him (17:9, 18). His prayer was not for the first disciples alone but for all who would believe through their witness. The reason for such unlimited provision is the scope of the mission (17:20-21). Too much is at stake for us to ignore the ministry of the Holy Spirit, who has been given to empower the church to fulfill our God-given mission.

Abundant Provision Evidenced in Acts

In the very first verse of Acts 1, Luke, the author, makes it clear that Jesus' ministry continues through the Spirit-empowered church. The first account, Luke's Gospel, was about "all that Jesus began to do and teach." Therefore, the Acts account is about all that Jesus continues to do as the ascended Lord. As commanded, the disciples were waiting for what the Father promised (v. 4), the baptism with the Holy Spirit, which would provide the power for the unlimited mission that would stretch to the remotest part of the earth (vv. 4, 6, 8).

In Acts 2 Pentecost signifies the spiritual ignition of the church and is accompanied by various signs such as "wind" and "fire." The wind reminds us of the promise of Ezekiel 37 where the "wind" animated the dead bones and created a mighty army. The fire throughout the Old Testament was a symbol of God's presence. The miracle that enabled each man to hear in his own language (v. 6) was the reversal of the events at Babel, and it was a clear indication that the gospel would be preached to every nation and tribe.

The key evidence of the empowering of the Spirit was the preaching of Peter, and the immediate conviction prompted by the Spirit, as more than three thousand souls were added to the church in a single day (vv. 37, 41). Effective evangelism was not the exception but the rule as "the Lord was adding to their number day by day those who were being saved" (v. 47). Peter and John were arrested for proclaiming the gospel but not until many believed, bringing the number of men to about five thousand (4:4). When asked about the source of their power, Peter (filled with the Holy Spirit) declared Jesus with such authority that the scribes and the Jewish authorities recognized that Peter and John had been with Jesus (v. 13).

Bold witness is clear evidence of the fullness of the Spirit (vv. 31, 33). The book of Acts follows the expansion of the gospel from Jerusalem to Judea to Samaria and to the uttermost part of the earth, ending with Paul in Rome. The Spirit-empowered witnesses were upsetting the world (17:6). The clearest proof of the resurrection is the church—made up of Jew and Gentile, slave and free, male and female—sharing community and taking the gospel to the very ends of the earth.

Unlimited Provision Taught by Paul

Paul planted most of the churches we read about in the New Testament. His letters to them give us critical insight into understanding their life and work. These churches and their people were anything but perfect. In most letters Paul found it necessary to bring correction and discipline. Nonetheless these young communities evangelized the known world in a short period of time.

Paul consistently urged early Christians to live up to their high calling and appropriate all that was available to them to live abundantly and expand God's kingdom on earth. He began his letter to the Corinthians by thanking God for the grace they had received, which had enriched them in everything so they were not lacking in any gift (1 Cor. 1:4-7). He declared that our human senses are not adequate to comprehend "all that God has prepared for those who love Him" (2:9). Yet the Christian can know and experience "the things freely given to us by God," because we have received the Spirit of God (vv. 11-12).

While Paul was required to correct misunderstandings about the meaning and function of the spiritual gifts, he nonetheless affirmed that God has gifted each person for the common good of the body of Christ (12:7), and He has placed the members in the body by His own design (v. 18).

In 2 Corinthians Paul spoke passionately about the provision

God has made for His church, enabling it to accomplish its divine mission. "And God is able to make all grace abound to you, so that always having all sufficiency in everything, you may have an abundance for every good deed" (9:8). This passage is found in a section that was written to motivate the Corinthians to complete an offering intended to assist the saints in Jerusalem who were suffering from famine. But the issue Paul addressed was much larger than giving; it was about living. Notice the repetition of "all," "everything," and "every." There is nothing lacking in God's provision. He supplies seed to the sower, multiplies the seed, and increases the harvest so that "you will be enriched in everything" (vv. 10-11).

Paul wrote the letters to the Ephesians, Colossians, and Philemon from his Roman prison cell. The church was beginning to face heretical teachings that diminished the uniqueness of Christ and thus challenged the significance of the church. A key Greek word in these companion letters is *pleroma*, translated "fullness." In Colossians 1:19 Paul said that God was pleased to have all the fullness of God to dwell in Christ. In the Ephesian letter, Paul boldly used this same term to speak of the church.

In Ephesians 1:18-23 Paul prayed that his readers of every generation would understand that we have been uniquely called by God to join Him in His kingdom activity. Further, Paul desired that we understand that God views us as His own unique people, His special heritage. But Paul's primary desire is that we would grasp the greatness of God's power that is available to us as we join Him in His mission. He then affirmed that these spiritual realities are made available to us by the strength of God, which had the power to raise Jesus from the dead. Christ, Paul declared, is now seated on God's right hand in the heavenly places with every authority in subjection to Him for the church. The church is "His body, the fullness of Him who fills all in all" (v. 23). The church is designed and empowered to express God's fullness (*pleroma*) in the world today as Jesus did during His days on earth through the incarnation.

This theme is picked up again in 3:10 where Paul declared that it was God's eternal purpose to reveal His "manifold wisdom" through the church. It reoccurs at the end of chapter 3 when Paul again turned to prayer, asking that his readers would be strengthened with power, know the love of Christ, and be filled up to all the fullness (*pleroma*) of God (vv. 14-19).

> **The church is designed and empowered to express God's fullness in the world today.**

I can think of no other way to conclude this chapter on unlimited provision than the benediction of Paul's prayer.

> Now to Him who is able to do far more abundantly beyond all that we ask or think, according to the power that works within us, to Him be the glory in the church and in Christ Jesus to all generations forever and ever. Amen. (Eph. 3:20-21)

The church of the Lord Jesus Christ is the recipient of unlimited resources, which are more than sufficient for the task of reaching our neighbors and the nations. It is a miracle beyond comprehension that God allows us to be the conduit for His miraculous unlimited power. It is the power that "works within us" that will bring glory to the church and Christ Jesus!

TRUTHS TO PONDER

1. Jesus' death and resurrection ushered in a new era of Kingdom activity where His followers were given unlimited resources to complete His kingdom agenda.

2. God created everything with intentionality to enable us to participate in Kingdom activity.

3. God's abundant provision is related to our stewardship of that which we have already been given.

4. Obedience to God's Word and involvement in His mission are closely tied to experiencing His unlimited provision.

5. Jesus' ministry illustrates His total reliance on His Father's unlimited resources.

6. The indwelling Holy Spirit is God's unlimited provision that enables us to participate meaningfully in fulfilling the Great Commission.

7. God's desire that we join Him in His kingdom activity is a wonderful mystery.

---

1 For a more detailed look at this section, see my book, *The Names of God* (Nashville: Broadman and Holman, 2001), 79-90.

2 If you desire to study the Kingdom impact of the Lord's Prayer in greater detail, see my book, *The Prayer of Jesus* (Nashville: Broadman Press, 2001). Prayer Journals, study guides, and video teaching aids are available from Auxanopress.com.

6

UNLIMITED PRESENCE

// "I am with you always, even to the end of the age." Can you imagine the impact those final words must have had on the first-century disciples? The emotional roller coaster they had experienced in recent days had been turbulent. They had been grieved by the crucifixion of the one they believed to be the Messiah. They were startled but encouraged by Jesus' resurrection appearances, and yet some were still doubtful (Matt. 28:17). They had been humbled and overwhelmed by the idea that they were to complete His mission of discipling the nations. The promise of His unlimited presence may have been both heartening and confusing. How could He be with them always?

Presence is powerful! My childhood bedroom was in the back of the house. A weeping willow tree grew not far from my window. Our security light was behind the tree, which meant that the shadow of those willowy branches often invaded my room. When the wind would howl, those branches would create a cast of shadowy creatures that would run across the floor and duck under my bed. I would call out to my dad, and he would shout back words of encouragement. While that helped, it didn't compare with his presence. When he opened the door and sat on the side of my bed, all the creatures were banished from sight. All was well!

The Old Testament Witness to God's Presence

The truth of God's personal presence is unique to Israel's religion and is clearly evidenced throughout the Old Testament narrative. Since the Bible is God's self-revelation, it is important to note that He wanted humankind, created in His image, to know that He was not an impersonal distant deity who was unconcerned and untouched by their needs and pains; He was always with them.

A unique aspect of Israel's religion was that their God was a movable God. He was not made by hands nor was He dependent upon man to move Him from place to place as were the idols. He was a God who was with His people. The idea of an omnipotent God is awesome to consider, but the assurance that He is "always" present is personal, intimate, comforting, and encouraging.

Humans Created to Enjoy God's Presence

There is something very personal about the creation account when God declared His intention of making man in His own image, according to His likeness (Gen. 1:26-27). Humankind, male and female, is the zenith of all creation and is given charge over all else. Humans begin life with the breath and blessing of God.

God created man as a relational being who needed and desired companionship. "Then the LORD God said, 'It is not good for the man to be alone; I will make him a helper suitable for him'" (Gen. 2:18). Out of man's rib woman was created to complement and complete man. They were to have such close communion that they would become one flesh.

But man's need and desire for companionship extended beyond that provided by human presence; man needed and enjoyed God's presence. Genesis 3:8 indicates that prior to their sinful rebellion the humans had enjoyed the physical presence of God, who was pictured as walking in the garden in the cool of the day. After their rebellion "the man and his wife hid themselves from the presence of the LORD God among the trees of the garden."

It is naïve to think that one can hide from the Creator, who is by nature without limits in His presence and knowledge; but sin makes us foolish enough to think we can fool God concerning our sin and escape His presence. Adam and Eve were driven from the garden for their own protection but not from the presence of God.

> God's redemptive plan is to redeem humanity, restoring the image of God in us and enabling us to live eternally in His presence.

God, faithful to His own character, remained with Adam and his descendants—guiding, protecting, and blessing His people.

God's redemptive plan is to redeem humanity, restoring the image of God in us and enabling us to live eternally in His presence.

The Period of the Patriarchs

We have already seen that the patriarchal period began with the call to Abram, which was punctuated throughout with the phrase "I will." Abram was called to leave his familiar homeland and journey to an unspecified destination. He did not need a detailed map because he had been assured of God's personal presence and direction—"I will show you." It is clear that God is not a distant unengaged deity. He promised to show Abram the way, to bless Abram and make His name great, and to protect him as he traveled by blessing those who blessed him and cursing those who cursed him (Gen. 12:1-3).

Abram began his journey as God commanded, and when he arrived in Shechem, the ever-present Lord appeared to Him with the reassuring words, "To your descendants I will give this land" (v. 7). When Lot chose to separate himself from Abram, God reassured Abram of His plan to make him a great nation and to give him the land (13:14-18). When Abram confessed his fear concerning God's promise to make him a great nation based on his and Sarai's childless condition, God reminded Abram that it was He who brought Abram out of Ur of the Chaldeans to give him the land (15:7). Simply stated, God reminded Abram of His abiding and guiding presence.

We discussed in the Unlimited Resources chapter that when Abram was ninety-nine years old God reaffirmed His covenant with him and changed both Abram and Sarai's names. Abram, meaning "exalted father," was changed to Abraham, "father of a multitude," and Sarai's name was changed to Sarah, "mother of nations" (Gen. 17:1-8, 15-16). In a sense God was enlarging a promise that must have already seemed impossibly large, since Abraham and Sarah were elderly and had no children. The messenger of the Lord asked Abraham a question that speaks to God's abundant provision through His unlimited presence—"Is anything too difficult for the LORD?" (18:14). Within a year, Isaac, the son of promise, was born.

The greatest challenge to Abraham's faith in God's presence and provision occurred when God instructed him to take Isaac, his only son, to Mount Moriah and offer him as a sacrifice. The conversation between father and son is instructive and is drawn to the reader's attention by the repetition of the phrase "So the two of them walked on together" (22:6, 8). When Isaac asked his father about the lamb for the sacrifice, Abraham simply replied, "God will provide for Himself the lamb for the burnt offering, my son" (v. 8). The word translated "provide" is the Hebrew word *jireh*, which can also be translated as "see." This term will later be placed in combination with the name *Jehovah*, meaning "the Lord will provide" (v. 14). The Lord's presence and His provision are inextricably bound together. The Lord who was present with Abraham saw and met his need.

Later, when Abraham was seeking a bride for Isaac, he sent his servant off with the assurance, "The LORD, before whom I have walked, will send His angel with you to make your journey successful" (24:40). The phrase "before whom I have walked" indicates that Abraham possessed an acute awareness of God's presence. For that reason, Abraham was confident that God's messenger would be with his servant. Years later, when Isaac was faced with a famine in the land, God instructed him not to go to Egypt but to remain in the land assured of His presence and provision (26:1-5).

This theme of God's guiding and providing presence was experienced from generation to generation. When Isaac sent Jacob to Paddan-aram to take a wife from the daughters of Laban, Jacob had a dream of a ladder set on the earth with its top extending to heaven. Angelic messengers were ascending and descending on it with the Lord standing above it, reaffirming His promise first given to Abraham to give him the land, to make him a great nation, and to enable him to bless the families of the earth. God promised, "Behold, I am with you and will keep you wherever you go, and will bring you back to this land; for I will not leave you until I have done what I have promised you" (28:12-15).

Jacob awoke and made a vow to God that included a commitment to return to Him a tenth of all He had provided. The words of Jacob's vow reflected the understanding that God would be with him, keep him, and provide for him on his journey (vv. 20-22).

After Jacob had served Laban for a lengthy period of time, God commanded him to return to the land of his relatives. It is noteworthy that Jacob was concerned that his brother, Esau, might kill him upon his return since he had stolen his birthright and blessing. Jacob was reassured by a single promise—"I will be with you" (31:3). The night before he was to encounter Esau, Jacob wrestled all night with a messenger of God. Understanding the importance of this messenger's presence, Jacob refused to let the messenger go until he blessed him (32:26). The messenger blessed Jacob and changed his name to Israel.

Even though Israel's beloved son Joseph was sold into Egypt

by his jealous brothers, God's plans and purposes were not thwarted by the brothers' evil actions (37:18-28; cf. 50:20). Joseph quickly experienced success in Egypt. "The LORD was with Joseph, so he became a successful man" (39:2). After Joseph ascended to the head of Potiphar's house, he was thrown into jail on a trumped up charge. Joseph was put in charge once again in the king's prison because, "The LORD was with Joseph and extended kindness to him, and gave him favor in the sight of the chief jailer" (vv. 21, 23).

Joseph was later released from jail to interpret the dream of the pharaoh, and he predicted seven years of plenty followed by seven years of famine. The pharaoh recognized that God had enabled Joseph to interpret the dream, and he set Joseph over the land of Egypt (41:38-41). In due time, the famine impacted Joseph's entire family. But Joseph was in a position to provide for them, and he instructed his brothers to bring their father and the entire family to Egypt. God instructed Israel to leave the promised land and make the journey. He was once again fortified by the promise of God's presence: "I will go down with you to Egypt, and I will also surely bring you up again; and Joseph will close your eyes" (46:4).

Throughout the period of the patriarchs we see the awareness of God's promised presence. His presence was the assurance of His provision and required the radical obedience of His people who were called to move at His command.

Moses and Joshua

The pharaoh who knew Joseph died, and the Israelites were forced into slavery in Egypt. The ever-present God saw their needs and "took notice of them" (Ex. 2:25). God uniquely pre-pared Moses, a Hebrew raised by Pharaoh's daughter (v. 10), to lead His people from captivity.

God made His presence known to Moses by means of a burn-ing bush and identified Himself as the God of the patriarchs (3:1-6). He assured Moses that He had seen the affliction of His people, given heed to their cries, and was prepared to deliver them and return them to a land of full provision that flowed with milk and honey (vv. 7-8).

God called and commissioned Moses to be the instrument of His deliverance, but Moses responded that he was neither wor-thy nor capable to accomplish the task (v. 11). God assured Mo-ses, "Certainly I will be with you, and this shall be the sign to you that it is I who have sent you: when you have brought the people out of Egypt, you shall worship God at this mountain" (v. 12). When Moses complained about his inability to speak, God responded "I, even I, will be with your mouth, and teach you what you are to say" (4:12). God's presence is the assurance of His full provision for those who join Him in His mission activity.

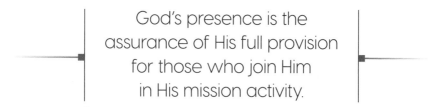

God's presence is the assurance of His full provision for those who join Him in His mission activity.

God provided a visible sign of His unlimited presence as the people exited Egypt and joined Him on the return journey to the promised land. "The LORD was going before them in a pillar of cloud by day to lead them on the way, and in a pillar of fire by night to give them light, that they might travel by day and by light. He did not take away the pillar of cloud by day, nor the pillar of fire by night, from before the people" (13:21-22). God not only delivered the Israelites at the Red Sea, He provided water and food for their travels (chs. 15–17). The apostle Paul, writing to the Corinthians, indicated that the spiritual drink God provided through the spiritual rock that followed them was Christ present with them (1 Cor. 10:4).

To assure Moses of His abiding presence, God promised that he would bring him and the Israelites to Mount Sinai to worship Him (Ex. 3:12). In the third month they camped in front of the mountain, and Moses went up to God where God gave him a message for Israel: "You yourselves have seen what I did to the Egyptians, and how I bore you on eagles' wings, and brought you to Myself" (19:4). It was not simply that God had rescued His people from bondage. He brought them to Himself. He is no distant impersonal deity—He wanted them safe, and He wanted them in His presence.

Even more, He wanted the Israelites to join Him in His kingdom activity. They were to obey His voice and keep His covenant so that they would be His unique possession, a kingdom of priests, and a holy nation (19:5-6). This "if—then" covenant shows the unique interrelationship between God's activity and humanity's response. They were to be His possession "among all the peoples, for all the earth is Mine" (v. 5). God's plan was to move His unique, holy, priestly people "among all the peoples" so that they might join Him in reclaiming the earth. The phrase "for all the earth is Mine" is not simply a statement of fact, but it is a missional mandate. God redeemed Israel to join Him in reclaiming all the peoples of the earth for His kingly rule. They were to accomplish this mission based on His abiding presence. God instructed the people to construct a sanctuary, "that I may dwell among them" (Ex. 25:8). The movable tabernacle was to be a visible and daily reminder of His unlimited presence among them. The ark of the covenant with the mercy seat on top would be the place where they would uniquely experience His presence and the leaders would hear His voice (v. 22). Everything about the tabernacle was indicative of the presence of Holy God among His people. "I will meet there with the sons of Israel, and it shall be consecrated by My glory . . . I will dwell among the sons of Israel and will be their God. They shall know that I am the Lord their God who brought them out of the land of Egypt, that I might dwell among them; I am the Lord their God" (29:43, 45-46).

One of the most grievous of Israel's sins occurred at the foot of Mount Sinai while Moses was on the mountain receiving the commandments that were to govern God's special people. When Moses delayed to come down from the mountain, the people assembled about Aaron and requested, "Come, make us a god who will go before us" (32:1b). Israel exchanged the God who had carried them from Egypt for a god they were required to carry. When Moses petitioned God for the lives of Israel, He again commissioned Moses to lead the people based on His presence, but He told Moses that He must punish those who had sinned (v. 34).

God reaffirmed His commitment to give Israel the land He had promised. He would send an angel or messenger before them, but He would not go up in their midst because of their obstinate unbelief (33:3). God's removal of His immediate presence was His loving protection so that Holy God would not destroy an unholy people. The restriction concerning His presence is similar to God's expulsion of Adam and Eve from the garden for their own protection.

This narrative raises the question of how an omnipresent God can remove His presence. First, we should note that throughout Scripture there are degrees of God's presence. For example, God was with Moses (v. 11) or with the Levites in a different way than He is simply present at all times with all people. Perhaps we should refer to this as God's *missional presence*, His empowering presence for those who are obedient to His mission.

Second, it was the disobedience of Israel that caused them to forfeit this direct missional presence. Later, in Numbers 20:8-12, we see a similar removal of missional presence when Moses, in his anger, struck the rock rather than speaking to it as God commanded. As a result, Moses was not allowed to enter the promised land with God's people. When Saul rebelled against God, we are told that God was with David but had departed from Saul (1 Sam. 18:12). Saul's anointing as king was removed, and his later days were spent in fruitless rebellion.

In the book of Revelation, the Lord speaks of having to remove the lampstand from the church of Ephesus unless they repent and do the deeds that they did at first (2:5). It is possible for people and churches to forfeit God's missional presence by the failure to obediently join Him on mission.

Returning to our narrative, Moses again interceded on behalf of the people, and God reaffirmed His presence and provision: "My presence shall go with you, and I will give you rest" (Ex. 33:14). Moses understood clearly what was at stake and responded, "If your presence does not go with us, do not lead us up from here" (v. 15). The presence of the one true God distinguished Israel "from all the other people who are upon the face of the earth" (v. 16). God, faithful to His own character assured Moses of His presence and His rest.

The Israelites stood poised to enter the promised land. At God's direction, twelve spies, one representative from each tribe, were sent into the land to see the good land that God was going to give them (Num. 13:1). The spies returned with the report that the land was so abundant it flowed with milk and honey (v. 27). Ten of them spoke of the strong people who inhabited the land and the fortified cities. They were convinced that the people in the land were too strong and could not be overtaken (vv. 28, 31). They were paralyzed with fear because they were attempting to accomplish God's mission in their own strength.

> It is possible for people and churches to forfeit God's missional presence by the failure to obediently join Him on mission.

Caleb and Joshua had a different assessment of the situation based on their understanding of God's powerful presence to give them the land: "If the LORD is pleased with us, then He will bring us into this land and give it to us—a land which flows with milk and honey. Only do not rebel against the LORD; and do not fear the people of the land, for they will be our prey. Their protection has been removed from them, and the LORD is with us; do not fear them" (14:8-9).

Instead of believing that God's powerful presence would

bring them victory, the people listened to the faithless spies and refused to take the land. The next morning, Israel awakened to the stark reality of the consequences of their sin and volunteered to go into the land (v. 40). Moses declared that they would not succeed, "for the LORD is not among you" (v. 42). Their rebellion against God's missional command resulted in the loss of His missional presence and empowering (v. 43). Some went up without Moses or the ark of the covenant and were beat down. As a result of their disobedience an entire generation doomed itself to fruitless wandering in the wilderness.

Moses' last task was to prepare the next generation to enter the land. He urged Israel to obey the statutes and judgments that God gave them so that they could possess the land He was giving them (Deut. 4:1). Moses' assurances that they would be able to possess the land were based on the unique character of their God. "For what great nation is there that has a god so near to it as the LORD our God whenever we call on Him?" (v. 7). God's unlimited presence distinguished Israel from all other people.

The fact that God chose Joshua as the man who would lead Israel into the promised land was hardly surprising. After all, he was one of the two spies who urged Israel to take the land based on God's promise and presence. You might wonder what would give Joshua the courage to succeed Moses and to accomplish the task Moses was unable to complete. No doubt it was the charge and assurance given to him by God: "No man will be able to stand before you all the days of your life. Just as I have been with Moses, I will be with you; I will not fail you or forsake you" (Josh. 1:5). God commanded Joshua to be careful to do according to all that is written in the word so that he would be successful in fulfilling his mission. "Have I not commanded you? Be strong and courageous! Do not tremble or be dismayed, for the LORD your God is with you wherever you go" (1:9).

We could list countless other greats of the Old Testament who were obedient and successful because they relied on God's presence. Gideon, a reluctant judge who was required to reduce the size of his army, was assured by God's promise, "Surely I will be with you, and you shall defeat Midian as one man" (Judg. 6:16). Jeremiah, concerned by his young age, was assured by God's promise: "Do not be afraid of them, / For I am with you to deliver you" (Jer. 1:8). David, a shepherd boy, volunteered to fight the Philistine giant Goliath based on his awareness of the presence of God, who had delivered him from the lion and the bear (1 Sam. 17:37). Daniel, a young man taken from his home country, could faithfully serve God in a pagan court because He was assured that the ever-present God had come in response to his prayers (Dan. 10:12).

The Psalmist's Testimony of God's Presence

Perhaps no other psalm is as loved as is Psalm 23. This psalm of David has the ring of personal testimony. "It speaks of a faith so-bered by trials and a life mellowed and matured by the passing of years . . . David had experienced conflict, both internal and external, that included war, family dissolution, personal disap-pointments, discouragement, and despair that would equal or exceed the experiences of any of us today."[1] Through it all, the king who was a great warrior had discovered God as his tender shepherd. Remember that God had called David from tending the sheep in the pasture to anoint him as the future king. Thus, in this psalm, as David contemplated God's care, he compared Him to a shepherd.

What stands out most throughout Psalm 23 is the presence of the shepherd with his sheep. It was his Shepherd's presence that assured David that he would experience full provision—"I shall not want" (v. 1). Every phrase speaks of the shepherd's presence, provision, and protection. "He makes me lie down . . . He leads . . . He restores . . . He guides" (vv. 2-3). In the shadowy valley of death, He is with me (v. 4). The preparation of the table, the anointing with oil, and the overflowing cup all speak of abundant provision based on personal presence (v. 5). The final phrase, "I will dwell in the house of the LORD forever," speaks of eternal unlimited presence (v. 6).

Psalm 139 expresses God's unlimited presence with great beauty:

> Where can I go from Your Spirit?
> Or where can I flee from Your presence?
> If I ascend to heaven, You are there;
> If I make my bed in Sheol, behold, You are there.
> If I take the wings of the dawn,
> If I dwell in the remotest part of the sea,
> Even there Your hand will lead me,
> And Your right hand will lay hold of me." (vv. 7-10)

A Prophetic Promise

The prophet Ezekiel was among those taken into Babylonian captivity. God used him to put this catastrophic event into historical perspective and give Israel a hope for the future. Through Ezekiel God promised a new day of fruitfulness for His name's sake (Eze. 36:22-38). Even though rebellious Israel had become like a valley of dry bones, when animated by the Spirit, they would once again become a mighty army (ch. 37).

Perhaps the greatest word of hope from Ezekiel is found in the final chapters of his book where we read about God's plan for the restoration of His people. Many of the plans are related to the rebuilding of the temple. The temple had been the most visible symbol of God's presence, but now it lay in ruins. The purpose for the reconstruction is stated in 43:4-5 where Ezekiel spoke of the glory of the Lord filling the house. Ezekiel's use of the phrase "God's glory" was a way of speaking of His presence. But the most encouraging word is found in the very last verse of Ezekiel—"and the name of the city from that day shall be, 'The LORD is there'" (48:35). That is the name *Jehovah Shammah*. Once again, God's powerful presence will be known among Israel.

The New Testament Witness to God's Presence

The Old Testament finds its ultimate fulfillment in the pages of the New Testament. The New Testament begins with the wonderful story of the coming of the Messiah, the rightful King. In Jesus, God's presence will be known in the flesh.

Immanuel Is God with Us

Matthew begins with a genealogy that introduces Jesus as the Messiah, the son of David, the son of Abraham (1:1). Matthew places Jesus squarely into the entire scope of Old Testament history. By tracing His lineage through the royal line, it solidified

Jesus' claim to the title "King of the Jews." But it is Matthew's use of the name Immanuel from Isaiah 7:14 that is of greatest interest to us.

An angel of the Lord appeared to Joseph to assure him that the child conceived in Mary was of the Holy Spirit and that he would be called Jesus (Matt. 1:20-21). *Jesus* is the Greek form of the name Joshua, meaning "Yahweh is salvation." This explains the angel's statement, "He will save His people from their sins."

Next, the angel explained that these events took place to fulfill Isaiah's promise about the miraculous birth of a child that would bring God's presence to humanity—Immanuel. It is not that Jesus ever bore Immanuel as an actual name but that He fulfilled the role of Immanuel. Jesus was God with us, and His ministry as Savior enables Him to bring sinful man fully into the presence of Holy God. Further, Matthew saw Immanuel as indicative of Jesus' person and His work. When Jesus healed or cast out demons, it was God at work through Jesus. The last name of the Old Testament—*Jehovah Shammah*—is fulfilled in the birth of Jesus, who is Immanuel.

John begins his Gospel by vaulting us back to the time before time began with the affirmation, "In the beginning was the Word, and the Word was with God, and the Word was God" (1:1). Further, John affirmed, "And the Word became flesh, and dwelt among us, and we saw His glory, glory as of the only begotten from the Father, full of grace and truth" (v. 14). In the Old Testament God's presence was seen in glorious display in the pillar of fire and pillar of cloud, in the mountain that glowed with His presence, and in the cloud that filled the temple. Now God's glory is fully expressed in Jesus, His person and ministry.

God's Presence Encountered through Jesus' Ministry

One of the early healing miracles recorded by John is in chapter 5 when Jesus healed the man at Bethesda. After the man was healed he told the Jews that Jesus had made him well. The Jews were persecuting Jesus because He was doing these things on the Sabbath. Jesus' response is telling—"My Father is working until now, and I Myself am working" (v. 17). In other words, Jesus had not initiated the healing of the lame man but had simply participated in what the Father was doing. The Jews understood fully what was at stake, and they now desired to kill Jesus because He "was calling God His own Father, making Himself equal with God" (v. 18).

Jesus' responded, "Truly, truly, I say to you, the Son can do nothing of Himself, unless it is something He sees the Father doing; for whatever the Father does, these things the Son also does in like manner. For the Father loves the Son, and shows Him all things that He Himself is doing; and the Father will show Him greater works than these, so that you will marvel" (vv. 19-20). Jesus' work was clear evidence of the Father's presence. The Father was at work through the Son.

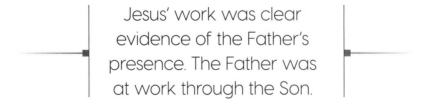

Jesus' work was clear evidence of the Father's presence. The Father was at work through the Son.

In the final days of Jesus' earthly ministry, He celebrated the Passover with His disciples. At this meal He spoke of His impending departure. After promising to prepare a place where He would bring them to Himself (John 14:3), Jesus spoke again of His oneness with the Father. Philip indicated that it would have been sufficient if He had shown them the Father (v. 8). He explained to Philip that those who had seen Him had seen the Father. "Do you not believe that I am in the Father, and the Father is in Me? The words that I say to you I do not speak on My own initiative, but the Father abiding in Me does His works" (v. 10). Even the words Jesus spoke came from the Father. The ministry and teaching of Jesus was sufficient proof of the Father's presence (v. 11).

Jesus' Physical Presence Replaced by His Abiding Presence through the Holy Spirit

The disciples were clearly concerned with what would happen to them between the time of Jesus' departure and His return to bring them into His eternal presence (cf. John 14:3). It was at this juncture that Jesus explained to His disciples that His leaving the earth would actually work to their advantage. First, He promised that because of His departure they would do greater works than He had accomplished during His brief earthly ministry (v. 12).

Not only did Jesus speak of the power of prayer uttered in His name (vv. 13-14), He spoke of another Helper that would be sent by the Father at the request of the Son. This Helper would be with them forever (v. 16). Jesus was speaking of the Holy Spirit, whom He first refers to as the Spirit of truth. The disciples will know Him precisely because "He abides with you and will be in you"

143

(v. 17). The Holy Spirit is the indwelling presence of Christ—"I will not leave you as orphans; I will come to you" (v. 18).

It is concerning that some evangelicals become nervous when discussing the ministry of the Holy Spirit. The Holy Spirit is one with the Father and the Son. He is sent by the Father at the request of the Son. He is the abiding presence of Christ in the life of the believer. He will be with us forever. He provides the power that enables us to bear much fruit for God's kingdom. He produces the fruit of the Spirit (Gal. 5:22-24) and distributes gifts for ministry to every believer (1 Cor. 12:7).[2] It may well be that a cause of our lack of power in fulfilling the Great Commission is our neglect of the ministry of the Spirit.

Next, Jesus contrasted His earthly ministry with the abiding work of the Spirit. "These things I have spoken to you while abiding with you. But the Helper, the Holy Spirit, whom the Father will send in My name, He will teach you all things, and bring to your remembrance all that I said to you" (John 14:25-26). The Holy Spirit enables us to understand and remember God's Word (cf. 16:12-15). This unique combination of the Spirit and the Word provides the necessary power for mission and ministry. When we rely on the Spirit to teach us and quicken our memories, it should have a profound effect on our preaching, teaching, and witnessing.

Jesus further illustrated the necessity of His abiding presence in the lives of His followers by speaking of Himself as the vine with His followers being the branches. His point is succinct and unequivocal, "Abide in Me, and I in you. As the branch cannot bear fruit of itself unless it abides in the vine, so neither can you unless you abide in Me. I am the vine, you are the branches;

he who abides in Me and I in him, he bears much fruit, for apart from Me you can do nothing" (15:4-5).

The two phrases, "cannot bear fruit of itself" (v. 4) and "apart from Me you can do nothing" (v. 5) should be crystal clear when taken together. A branch separated from the vine is fruitless. "Nothing" means precisely what it says. We need to turn to prayer more often than just when we hit a stumbling block and can't think of anything else to do on our own. We must constantly seek His presence and power through prayer since we can do *nothing* apart from His presence. We shouldn't rely on the Spirit just when we exhaust our human ingenuity and effort. We must be totally reliant upon His Spirit if we are to produce much fruit that endures.

While we can do *nothing* apart from His presence, we can agree with the apostle Paul who affirmed that it is God at work in us (Phil. 2:13), and therefore "I can do all things through Him who strengthens me" (4:13). The contrast between *nothing* and *all things* could not be more striking.

It is noteworthy that Jesus, in His final remarks to His disciples, reemphasized the importance of the indwelling of the Spirit and the Great Commission efforts of His followers. The promised Helper would testify about Jesus (John 15:26). Thus, witnessing becomes both natural and effective when empowered by the Spirit. Jesus reiterated His radical claim that His departure would be an advantage for the disciples since it enabled Him to send the Holy Spirit (16:7). In this context, we have a unique reference to the ministry of the Holy Spirit to the world. He convicts the world concerning sin and righteousness and judgment

(vv. 8-11). Simply stated, the effectiveness of our ministry depends upon the Spirit and not our own powerful rhetoric.

We need to remind ourselves again why this gift of presence is so critical. "As you sent Me into the world, I also have sent them into the world" (17:18). The Son was sent into the world to bring the good news of salvation that is available to all who would believe (3:16-17). Jesus expanded His prayer to include all persons who believe in Him through the witness of these first disciples with a singular bottom line goal, "so that the world may believe that You sent Me" (17:21). God's unlimited love is reflected in His unlimited atonement, which mandates an unlimited mission that requires the unlimited resources provided by His unlimited indwelling presence.

God's Presence and Our Ministry

The apostle Paul discovered that when he had persecuted the followers of Jesus he had actually been persecuting the Lord Himself (Acts 9:5). In converse manner, we must realize that when we minister to others in the name of Jesus we are ministering to Him. In the narrative of the judgment, the King invites those who have fed Him, given Him drink, clothed Him, and visited Him when sick and in prison to "inherit the kingdom prepared for you from the foundation of the world" (Matt. 25:34-36). The righteous responded by asking when they performed such acts for the King. "The King will answer and say to them, 'Truly I say to you, to the extent that you did it to one of these brothers of Mine, even the least of them, you did it to Me'" (v. 40).

As we minister to others we both *express* His presence and *experience* His presence. He is present, empowering our ministry, and He is present as a recipient of our ministry when we feed the poor, visit the sick, care for the downcast, and share the good news of God's love.

God's Presence for All Eternity

Let's visit John 17 for a final moment. After praying for the unity, joy, and sanctification of the disciples and those who will believe through their witness, Jesus made a final request of the Father concerning all those the Father has given to Him: "Father, I desire that they also, whom You have given Me, be with Me where I am, so that they may see My glory which You have given Me, for You loved Me before the foundation of the world" (v. 24). It is beyond comprehension that Jesus' final request, on the eve of His betrayal, was that we would enjoy His eternal presence and see His preexistent glory.

John wrote about this eternal presence in his final revelation: "And I heard a loud voice from the throne, saying, 'Behold, the tabernacle of God is among men, and He will dwell among them, and they shall be His people, and God Himself will be among them'" (Rev. 21:3). His eternal presence will put an end to tears, death, mourning, crying and pain (v. 4). John attempted to describe the resplendent beauty of heaven by using precious stones and metals. But the true beauty of heaven is the presence of the Lord God Almighty and the Lamb who illumine it with glory (vv. 18-23). Further, we see that the unlimited mission has been completed as the nations are healed and the kings of the earth bring their glory before the one true King (vv. 24-26).

Knowing that the Great Commission will be completed before the King returns (Matt. 24:14) should stir within us the desire to join God in seeing His kingdom come. The assurance of His presence should give us unlimited confidence that we can join God in His kingdom activity to every people group on the earth.

TRUTHS TO PONDER

1. A unique aspect of Israel's religion was God's unlimited presence among them.

2. God's presence is the assurance of His provision and calls for His people to join Him in His mission activity.

3. God's missional presence and empowering can be forfeited by unbelief or disobedience.

4. Jesus' ministry and teaching was a clear demonstration of His Father's presence.

5. The Holy Spirit is the abiding presence of Jesus in us and makes us fully capable of fulfilling the Great Commission. Our human inability is merely the platform for His unlimited ability.

6. The Holy Spirit informs our minds, heightens our memory, empowers our ministry, bears the fruit of the Spirit in our lives, and distributes gifts for ministry.

7. Through Kingdom activity we can *express* and *experience* God's presence.

*God's unlimited love is manifest
in His unlimited atonement, which
mandates an unlimited mission that
requires unlimited resources, fully
provided by His unlimited presence.*

Covenant to join Him today in
the reaching of the nations.

---

1 Ken Hemphill, *The Names of God* (Nashville: Broadman and Holman, 2001), 162-163.

2 For a more complete understanding of the role of gifts in Kingdom activity, see my book, *You Are Gifted: Your Spiritual Gifts and the Kingdom of God* (Nashville: B&H, 2009).

Auxano Press Non-Disposable Curriculum

- Designed for use in any small group
- Affordable, biblically based, and life oriented
- Choose your own material and stop and start times
- Study the Bible and build a Christian library

For teaching guides and additional small group study materials, or to learn about other Auxano Press titles, visit Auxanopress.com.

Auxano
PRESS

Other Books
by Ken Hemphill

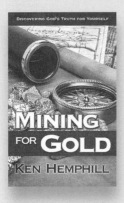

Do you believe God's truth is more precious than gold? Do you dig into God's Word with the same passion you would exert to find physical gold? Learn three different styles of reading and eight essential questions to ask of every text to help you discover the pure riches of God's Word.

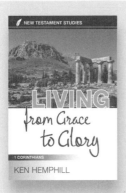

In 1 Corinthians Paul anchors the Christian life in the grace of God, affirming that our eyes, ears, and hearts have not yet comprehended all God has prepared. If you want to know what God has in store for you and your church, study *Living from Grace to Glory* and discover what you have to offer Christ through His church.

For teaching guides and additional small group study materials, or to learn about other Auxano Press titles, visit Auxanopress.com.